D1646104

The Mystery of the Incarnation

Books by Norman Anderson
published by Hodder and Stoughton

A LAWYER AMONG THE THEOLOGIANS

ISSUES OF LIFE AND DEATH

Contents

Foreword

I AM MOST GRATEFUL TO THE BISHOP JOHN PRIDEAUX
Memorial Trustees for inviting me to give this year's series of
lectures, and I am very conscious of the honour they
have done me. My predecessors in this assignment have all
been 'professionals' in some aspect of the many related
subjects to which the Trust is devoted, and they include some
outstanding names. I, by contrast, am an amateur in this field,
so the question might well be asked why I was foolhardy
enough to accept the invitation. To this my primary answer
would have to be that I could not resist the opportunity it gave
me to do some reading and thinking about a subject which
had for long fascinated me, but which the circumstances of a
busy and variegated life had hitherto prevented me from
studying in any detail. I comforted myself, moreover, by the
thought that there has been quite a vogue, in recent years, for
Universities occasionally to invite a speaker to address
himself to a subject in a discipline other than his own, in the
hope that this will not only provide an antidote to excessive
specialisation but may also help other laymen in their approach to the topic – and even, perhaps, prove of some
interest to the experts by giving them the chance to see it
through a layman's eyes.

Let me introduce this series of lectures, then, by attempting
to answer two initial questions:

(1) *Why devote these lectures to the Incarnation?*

Today the answer to this question may seem obvious, in the
light of the positive spate of recent publications on this
subject. But in point of fact I made my choice almost as soon
as I received the invitation; and I was compelled to start

preliminary work on them as long ago as the autumn of 1976 – partly because I wanted to use some of the basic material for a series of lectures I had to give in Australia in the following May, and partly because I knew I should have to divert my attention, well before that, to the preparation of the Hamlyn Lectures on 'Liberty, Law and Justice' which I was to give in Bristol in the same two weeks as the Prideaux Lectures, and which (unlike the latter) had to be published on the day when the last lecture was delivered. It was only when I wrote to Professor John Hick to ask if he would be kind enough to send me a copy of the Presidential Address he had given, in the Spring of 1976, to the Society for Theological Studies on 'Jesus and World Religions' that he told me he intended to include a somewhat amended version of this in a book entitled *The Myth of God Incarnate,* which he was currently editing and which was to be published in the following summer. Since then, as you will all know, a reply with the title of *The Truth of God Incarnate* was produced in what must be almost record time; and three other important books have been published on this subject: *The Origin of Christology,* by Professor C. F. D. Moule; *Theology and the Gospel of Christ,* by Professor E. L. Mascall (about half of which is devoted to Christology); and *God as Spirit* (The Bampton Lectures for 1976), by Professor G. W. H. Lampe. But let me quote some words I wrote about the Incarnation before I knew that any of these books were to be written:

'I believe that this subject is absolutely fundamental to the contemporary debate about Christianity, both inside and outside the Church. To those who are completely uncommitted but prepared to take the matter seriously, the burning question is whether the Christian faith can in fact be embraced today with intellectual integrity: and they are perfectly aware that this depends on whether they can accept the Christian claim that behind and beyond all the phenomena of nature and the baffling problems of human life there is an all-powerful and all-loving Being who was uniquely revealed, and

can still be personally known, in Jesus of Nazareth. To
those who profess and call themselves Christians, again,
it is the reality and meaning of the Incarnation which
constitute the basic point of current controversy and
debate. Theologians today are questioning the validity,
adequacy and relevance of the christological formulations in the Creeds, and are submitting their New
Testament basis to an exceedingly radical examination
in a way which often leaves the parochial clergy and
their parishioners bewildered, upset and even affronted
by what they read and hear.'

(2) *Why choose as title 'The Mystery of the Incarnation'?*

To this I would reply that I am aware that the word 'mystery' is
under severe criticism in the context of theological debate.
But I do not resort to this term because – to quote Stephen T.
Katz's strictures in his essay on 'The language and logic of
"mystery" in Christology'[1] – I believe that 'neither ordinary
language nor logic is relevant to theology'; that the subject is,
in principle, so insoluble that 'every sort of thing which might
conceivably be offered as a solution is denied *a priori*'; or that
it is impossible to discuss the Incarnation in a way which is
both intelligible and meaningful. On the contrary, a number
of recent books and essays on this subject have been eminently lucid and down to earth. So I use the word 'mystery' not
because I wish to 'don the mantle of the mystery devotee' but
simply because I believe it expresses, better than any other
term, the fact that we are here face to face with a subject
which, by its very nature, the human mind can never fully
fathom. But this does not mean that we are in any way exempt
from wrestling with it, nor does it excuse any flight into
woolliness of thought or obscurity of language.

Would not the word 'problem', then, prove a preferable
alternative? It would certainly fit more naturally into much of
the contemporary debate, which often (though by no means
always) seems to savour primarily of a rigorous quest for the

[1]   In *Christ, Faith and History* (ed. S. W. Sykes and J. P. Clayton, C.U.P. 1972).

solution to a baffling intellectual puzzle. But I believe that the Incarnation is much more than this, and that any attempt to understand it demands spiritual sensitivity, and even awe, as well as theological learning and intellectual acumen.

Another possible term in this context would be the word 'paradox' – as favoured, for example, by D. M. Baillie in *God was in Christ,* and criticised by R. W. Hepburn in *Christianity and Paradox.* Like mystery, this would certainly suggest that the Incarnation is a subject which cannot be reduced to a purely logical formula, fitted into ready-made categories, or resolved by reference to known precedents. According to one meaning listed in the *Shorter Oxford English Dictionary,* moreover, the term paradox describes something which is 'seemingly self-contradictory or absurd, though possibly well-founded or essentially true'. But the term is, we are told, 'often applied to a proposition which is actually self-contradictory, and so essentially absurd or false'. I have opted, therefore, for 'mystery' because I believe the Incarnation is the most meaningful event that has ever happened, though we certainly cannot fully understand it with our finite minds, and because the word seems to me eminently suitable to a subject which is not primarily baffling and elusive but unfathomable and numinous.

I could, of course, very well have substituted the term 'Christology' for 'the Incarnation'. In some ways this might, in fact, have been preferable, for I shall certainly not be concerned exclusively with the period of Christ's earthly life. But to speak of the Incarnation seems much more appropriate in the context of comparative religion, for example; and it clearly embraces, or at least suggests, the exaltation of the risen Christ and the doctrine of his pre-existence.

This year's series of Bishop John Prideaux Lectures were given in the University of Exeter at the end of February and the beginning of March. I should add that only four of the six chapters in this book were actually given as lectures. The second chapter, which is merely a summary of the christological controversies of the past, has been added for the convenience of those readers who are not familiar with this aspect of the history of Christian doctrine; and I omitted the first of the two chapters entitled 'Some Examples of the Contemporary Debate'.

In conclusion, I should like to express my sincere gratitude for much kindness and hospitality on the part of the staff and students of the University of Exeter and the clergy of Devon.

Cambridge, March 1978   NORMAN ANDERSON

1
The Background to the Contemporary Debate

I SUPPOSE THAT THE BASIC, AND PROBABLY THE EARLIEST, Christian confession of faith is the simple statement 'Jesus is Lord' – and that from this no truly Christian theologians of past or present would dissent, however 'orthodox', 'avant garde' or even 'heterodox' they may be considered. Controversy arises only when one starts to question what, precisely, this confession means, and what it implies in theory and practice. We shall begin to consider this, in general terms, in this chapter. Next, for the convenience of those who are not very familiar with the subject, I shall attempt to outline the christological controversies which led up to the Nicene Creed and the Definition of Chalcedon, those which followed in the next two or three centuries, and those which ensued in the Lutheran and Reformed traditions. I shall devote my third chapter to the Incarnation in the context of comparative religion, and the next two – 'Some Examples of the Contemporary Debate' – to a detailed examination of the christological views of a few representative theologians. Finally, in my last chapter, I shall try to draw the subject together and summarise my own conclusions.

As a broad generalisation, there are always two possible approaches to Christology – or, in terms of the way in which I have introduced the subject, to the confession that 'Jesus is Lord'. One can begin from one's doctrine of God and argue from that to Jesus, adopting a deductive or what may be described as a 'downward' approach. Alternatively, one can start from the Jesus of the Gospels and see whether he leads us to God, following an inductive or 'upward' approach. Obviously enough, both approaches are in fact needed; and

11

in the New Testament – and particularly, perhaps, in the Epistle to the Hebrews – they largely go hand in hand. But the first disciples necessarily began with Jesus, the man they knew so well as teacher and had come to accept as Messiah; and it seems to me that this is the natural starting point for us too.

What, then, are the basic facts? A great deal has been written in recent years about the titles applied to Jesus in the Gospels, whether by himself or others; but it would go beyond my purpose and my competence to attempt to evaluate the very different theories on this subject advocated by New Testament scholars. I will therefore hazard the dogmatic statement that I myself have no doubt whatever that Jesus repeatedly used the symbol 'Son of Man' – or, more accurately, '*The* Son of Man'[1]; that he applied it to himself rather than to someone else (often, perhaps, as an indirect way of saying 'I' or 'me'); and that, in whatever other sense he may have used it, he sometimes invested it with an apocalyptic meaning derived, in part, from Daniel 7. The suggestion that this title was imported, as it were, by the primitive Church, and put by the evangelists almost exclusively into his mouth, seems to me incredible on a number of different grounds – but particularly in view of the fact that it would have appeared so inadequate to them in the light of their Easter faith. It seems, moreover, that there is 'virtually no evidence' for the theory that it was first applied to Jesus by the post-resurrection Church,[2] whereas the phrase, if used by Jesus himself, would have enabled him, in the words of Professor G. B. Caird, 'without actually claiming to be Messiah, to indicate his essential unity with mankind, and above all with the weak and humble, and also his special function as predestined representative of the new Israel and bearer of God's judgment and Kingdom.[3]

But did Jesus in fact claim to be Messiah? I am myself

[1] Cf. C. F. D. Moule, *The Origin of Christology* (C.U.P. 1977), pp. 13-22.
[2] *Ibid.*, p. 20.
[3] *Commentary on St. Luke's Gospel* (The Pelican Gospel Commentaries, 1963), pp. 94f.

convinced that Professor C. H. Dodd was right when he wrote, in regard to the trial of Jesus:

> The evangelists, I conclude, John and the Synoptics alike, take the view that Jesus was charged with blasphemy because he spoke and acted in ways which implied that he stood in a special relation with God, so that his words carried divine authority and his actions were instinct with divine power. Unless this could be believed, the implied claim was an affront to the deepest religious sentiments of his people, a profanation of sanctities; and this, I suggest, is what the charge of "blasphemy" really stands for, rather than any definable statutory offence... Whether or not Jesus had put himself forward as Messiah, the implied claim was messianic at least, perhaps rather messianic plus.[4]

Indeed, I would myself be less cautious, and say that it seems clear that, while he did not use the title of himself in his public teaching (largely, I believe, because his Jewish contemporaries would have understood it in terms of those currents in Jewish thought that depicted the Messiah as a national deliverer or conquering king rather than those prophecies about the 'Suffering Servant' by which he himself chiefly interpreted his mission), he sometimes went distinctly further than merely to accept the title tacitly or make messianic claims by implication. At the climax of his ministry, moreover, 'the so-called triumphal entry (Mark 11) looks uncommonly like a deliberate messianic gesture or demonstration', Moule observes, but

> one so staged as to say, 'If I *am* Messiah, I am not going to fight the Romans, I am going to fight abuse at the heart of Judaism.' And finally, when it is clear that no violent action is possible, because Jesus is already a prisoner, he is represented, apparently, as acknowledging messiahship before the Sanhedrin (Mark 14:62).

---

[4] 'The Historic Problem of the Death of Jesus', in C. H. Dodd, *More New Testament Studies* (Manchester University Press, 1968).

So, he concludes,

> the tenacity of the usage is most plausibly ex-
> plained. . .if Jesus himself had accepted the royal title,
> but, during his ministry, had so radically reinterpreted
> it that it became natural to his followers to use it in this
> new way.[5]

In view of the statement in Deut. 21:23 that 'a hanged man
is accursed by God', moreover, it seems to me almost
incredible that Jewish Christians should have used this title
unless they 'believed that Jesus believed himself to be
Messiah',[6] and there seems to be no substance whatever in
the allegation that Jesus refused the title at Caesarea Philip-
pi. Instead, he gave his disciples, in the Marcan account,
'strict orders not to tell anyone about him' (which would
suggest that he accepted the title but did not want it to be
made public), while he is recorded, in the Matthean account,
as having told Peter that his confession 'You are the
Messiah, the Son of the living God', had been the result of a
revelation from 'my heavenly Father'.[7]

The addition of the words 'the Son of the living God' in
Matthew's account of Peter's confession inevitably raises
the question of the use and meaning of the title 'Son of God',
or simply 'the Son', when applied or attributed to Jesus in
the New Testament. In itself the title need have no deeper
significance than that of Messianic King[8]; and many participants in the contemporary debate about Christology
insist that the impact of Hellenistic belief in mythological
heroes and 'divine men',[9] Roman ascription of 'divinity' to
their Emperors, and Old Testament references to Israel's
Kings, Israel itself as a nation, and even the angels, as God's
'sons', naturally enough led the early Church, with its

[5]   *Op. cit.,* pp. 33f.
[6]   Cf. O. Cullmann, *The Christology of the New Testament* (SCM Press, London, 1959), p. 8.
[7]   Mark 8:30 and Matt. 16:17.
[8]   Cf. 2 Sam. 7:14 and Psalm 2:2 and 7.
[9]   e.g. *The Myth of God Incarnate* (SCM Press, London, 1977), pp. 100ff.

unbounded reverence for the Jesus it believed to be exalted to God's right hand, first to regard him as the 'Son of God' in a theological rather than metaphysical or poetic sense, and then to transform this concept into that of 'God the Son'. But does the evidence in fact support this theory?

Let us start, by way of illustration, with a point to which I shall not revert except in one or two passing references: namely, the Virgin Birth or, more precisely, the virginal conception. This is an article of faith included in all the Creeds and constantly repeated by the greater part of Christendom; but it is widely questioned today, and often denied, by many who would not by any means regard themselves as *avant garde*. It is, of course, manifestly true that the evidence for the Virgin Birth – to which unambiguous references in the New Testament are confined to the beginning of the first and third Gospels – is incomparably less strong than that for the resurrection, and that it does not seem to have represented any essential part of the apostolic *kerygma*. When, however, it is alleged that virgin-births are found in many pagan myths and religions, so it was almost inevitable that the Christian Church should come to believe that Christ, if divine, must have been born of a virgin – or even that he was divine because he had been born of a virgin – this is wide open to challenge. Pagan mythology, as Dr Alan Richardson rightly insists,

> is full of legends of a supernatural hero born of intercourse between a god and a human woman. But this is scarcely a *virgin* birth, and there is no real parallel to the story of the birth of Christ in pagan literature. The Jewish mind (and Matt. 1 and Luke 1 are intensely Jewish) would have been revolted by the idea of physical intercourse between a divine being and a woman.[10]

Similarly, any idea that the stories of the Virgin Birth

[10] *A Dictionary of Christian Theology* (ed. by Alan Richardson, SCM Press, London, 1969), pp. 357f.

owed their origin to any Gnostic or Manichaean notion that sexual intercourse was in itself sinful or unclean would have been wholly alien to Jewish thought. A much more plausible motive for the invention of such a legend, if legend it were, would have been the insistence of the early Church that Jesus had indeed 'come in the flesh': that he was truly 'born of a woman', and not a mere theophany. Nor can it be argued that the Church's belief in the sinlessness of Jesus is in any sense 'guaranteed' by the Virgin Birth, as the Roman Catholic dogma of the Immaculate Conception of Mary herself sufficiently testifies.

The truth is that both Matthew and Luke 'state the fact of Christ's birth of a virgin in a straightforward and un-argumentative way; they offer no hints as to why it should have happened thus and they draw no conclusions from it. So-called "theological" objections to the historicity of the Virgin Birth are based upon a reading into the narratives of motives that are not present in them', for the Gospel accounts 'simply relate an historical happening and leave the matter without any form of explanation'.[11] The absence of any mention of the Virgin Birth by any other New Testament writer, moreover, proves no more than the fact to which I have already referred, that it did *not* form part of the apostolic *kerygma*. It was something that those who already believed in Jesus were taught, not a ground on which they called others to faith.

But we must turn to broader issues. It is a fact, I think, that even radical critics commonly acknowledge the profound filial consciousness which characterised the Jesus of the Gospels. We may surmise, moreover, that the secret did not *primarily* lie in a subjective consciousness of his own identity, but in an intimate knowledge of God as his Father. In Father Louis Bouyer's words: 'We must not try to represent to ourselves this consciousness of Jesus, whether messianic or filial, as being essentially, and still less as being

[11] Alan Richardson, *An Introduction to the Theology of the New Testament* (SCM Press, London, 1958: fourth impression, 1969), pp. 171ff.

primarily, a reflex consciousness of its own identity'. That, he says, has been the common error of Christologies. But

> the difficulties which that starting point cannot avoid accumulating vanish as soon as we recognise that this consciousness of Jesus, like every normal consciousness, was the consciousness of an object before becoming a consciousness of its own subject. The consciousness of Jesus, as the human consciousness of the Son of God, was before all else consciousness *of God*. Jesus was 'the Christ, the Son of the living God', not directly by knowing that he was, but because he knew God *as the Father*... What is unique in the consciousness of Jesus of Nazareth is that it was pierced and traversed, from its first awakening, by that intuition, which was to precede, penetrate, and saturate all his states of consciousness, whatever they might be.[12]

And Père Galot makes the same point when he insists that 'When the Son humanly takes consciousness of himself, he does it as a Son, by taking consciousness of his relation to the Father. . .'[13]

Not only did he habitually refer to God as his Father, but it seems clear that it was his practice to address him by the Aramaic term 'Abba'. This was a child's word, Moule comments,

> and it seems to have been used in ordinary family life, but never (so far as our information goes) in direct address to God, except on the lips, first of Jesus, and then of Christians; and even Christians soon reverted to the standardised Jewish form 'our Father in heaven'. . . It looks, then, as though it was Jesus himself who first dared to use this very simple, family address

---

[12] *Le Fils éternel* (Paris, Cerf, 1974), p. 510 – as quoted by Mascall, *Theology and the Gospel of Christ* (SPCK, London, 1977), pp. 137 and 150.
[13] *La Conscience de Jésus* (Gembloux, Duculot; and Paris, Lethielleux, 1971), pp. 179f. – as quoted by Mascall, *op. cit.*, p. 167.

in his prayer to God. It is one of the three or four Aramaic words and phrases used in the traditions of the words of Jesus.[14]

When, moreover, we find St Paul using this same Aramaic word, 'gratuitously embedded in the alien texture' of two letters written in Greek to largely Gentile Churches, to describe how the Holy Spirit inspires even Greek-speaking Christians to pray, the retention of this term in its original form can, surely, only be regarded as an authentic – and very precious – memory of the historical Jesus himself. And it seems equally clear that it was a consciousness of this unique filial relationship that alone can explain the serene authority with which he habitually spoke and acted. This amazed his contemporaries; and it still strikes us today as at once paradoxical, yet in his case strangely natural, in one who could claim to be 'meek and lowly in heart' and who was, indeed, accepted by his disciples as such.

If Jesus in fact enjoyed such an intimate relationship with his Father, it is surely natural – and even inevitable – that he should sometimes have put it into words in his teaching as well as his prayers. It is hardly surprising, then, that Matthew records that he preceded his invitation to all who 'labour and are heavy laden' to come to him, the one who was himself 'meek and lowly in heart', for rest and instruction, by the statement that 'Everything is entrusted to me by my Father, and no one knows the Son but the Father, and no one knows the Father but the Son and those to whom the Son may choose to reveal him'.[15] Such statements are, of course, much more frequent in the Fourth Gospel, where their authenticity has been widely questioned as incongruous with the picture of Jesus we get from the Synop-

---

[14] C. F. D. Moule, *The Phenomenon of the New Testament* (SCM Press, London, 1967), pp. 63ff.

[15] Matt. 11:27; Luke 10:22. This represents one of those 'Q' passages which are often regarded as among the earliest strands in the traditions. But cf. also the inescapable implication in the parable of the wicked husbandmen.

tic records as a whole. But Professor R. V. G. Tasker aptly remarks that

> Though at times the utterances of Jesus in this Gospel sound harsh. . .there is no valid reason for supposing that, when dealing with the Rabbis at Jerusalem, he did not debate with them in rabbinical fashion the nature of his claims; and it may well be just this side of the Lord's ministry that the Galilean disciples knew little about, but with which the fourth Evangelist was more familiar, particularly if, as has already been suggested, he was himself a Jerusalem disciple.[16]

But, however this may be, we too easily forget that to call Jesus the 'Christ' or 'Messiah' after his crucifixion must have been a continual 'scandal' to Jews and that the title could scarcely have survived 'unless his friends had already become convinced that he was Messiah in some unusual and transcendental sense'. In other words, 'it is easier to trace a transcendental conception of the Son to something in Jesus's own life or person' – or, we might add, his teaching – 'than to account for the continued use, after the crucifixion, of the title Messiah, from which it is proposed to evolve a transcendental Sonship.'[17]

Much more could, of course, be written about the Gospel records as a whole. Instead of the time-honoured prophetic formula 'Thus saith the Lord' the Jesus of the Gospels – the Synoptics and John alike – is remembered as habitually introducing his teaching with the arresting words 'Amen, I say to you'. It was partly for this reason that the people were 'astonished', because 'unlike the doctors of the law, he taught with a note of authority'.[18] It is in this context that Professor A. M. Hunter insists: 'Search Jewish literature

[16] *The Nature and Purpose of the Gospels* (SCM Press, London, sixth impression, 1957), pp. 96f.
[17] Cf. C. F. D. Moule, 'Incarnation: paradox that will not go away' in T. H. E. S., 23 Dec. 1977.
[18] Mark 1:22 NEB.

and you will look in vain for a man who prefaces his words with "Amen, I say unto you", who dares to address God as Abba, who tells his disciples that he alone knows the Almighty as Father'.[19] Again, though he taught his disciples always to pray for forgiveness, there is no suggestion in the Gospel records that he himself had any sense of personal sin whatever – even forgiven sin. Instead, his fellowship with his 'Father' seems to have been uniformly close and unbroken, except only at the time of the 'cry of dereliction' on the cross. But side by side with this fellowship (and, no doubt, mediated by it) we find an ever-growing sense of his unique mission – a divine imperative which continually drove him on. And when the prospect of his own suffering and death came into view, he clearly interpreted this largely, in terms of Isaiah 53, as 'a ransom for many'; as a 'new covenant' sealed by his blood; and as the very essence 'of that for which he had come, and the heart of his mission and authority'.[20] It is obvious, moreover, that any understanding of what he did depends on who he was, and *vice versa*; for soteriology and Christology *cannot* be separated.

But to the end his disciples did not understand. They may have sensed, in some measure, what Professor H. E. W. Turner terms the 'hinterland of his divinity';[21] but what they knew without a semblance of doubt was that he was truly and unquestionably a man. There was much about him that they could not understand, and many of his statements were inexplicable to them at the time. In particular, his predictions of his coming sufferings fell on deaf ears, and when he was in fact crucified all their hopes were dashed in pieces. What is clear beyond any question is that it was his resurrection and exaltation, and this alone, which constituted the 'watershed' in primitive Christology. In a very real sense, indeed, it represented a wholly new beginning.

Nor is this difficult to understand. Far from 'redeeming Israel' in the way they had expected the Messiah would do,

[19] *Bible and Gospel* (SCM Press, London, 1969), p. 133.
[20] A. M. Ramsey, *God, Christ and the World* (SCM Press, London, 1969), p. 89.
[21] *Jesus the Christ* (Mowbray's, London, 1976), *passim*.

he had been betrayed and crucified, had died and been buried, in what must have seemed to them abject failure and disgrace. *But God had raised him from the dead*; and had thereby turned defeat into victory, and vindicated both his person and his work. On the first Easter morning the tomb was found to be empty; and before evening he had himself appeared to several of his disciples, alone or in groups. A number of unforgettable days had followed, in the course of which he had 'presented himself' to them, 'alive after his passion', in a way they subsequently described as 'many infallible proofs'. He was changed, indeed, for he now lived on a wholly different plane; yet he was unmistakably the same Jesus, whom they had known so well and could confidently identify, although they sometimes failed to recognise him at once. These 'appearances', moreover, could not be written off as visions, however vivid; for he had actually been 'handled' or touched, and on at least one occasion, we are told, he had given concrete evidence of his objective presence by eating a piece of fish. But though the risen Christ was no ghost or phantom, and could invite a finger to explore the print of the nails, he was very different from a resuscitated corpse, and was no longer subject to physical limitations.[22]

Those wonderful days, during which he came in and went out among them (and taught them something of the meaning of his life and, pre-eminently, of his death), had ended, as he had himself made clear by a visible withdrawal from their sight – for, with Dr. Michael Ramsay, I certainly accept this as a historical event. But they knew that he was now exalted 'to the right hand of God'. It seems probable, indeed, that from his point of view his exaltation or ascension had taken place on Easter day; and his disciples subsequently came to see even his crucifixion, in all its apparent shame and weakness, as part of his exaltation. But although he was no longer with them in the visible and objective manner of the 'forty days', yet he had not left them

[22] See below, p. 22, etc.

desolate or alone. On the contrary, he had promised that he would come to them in a new way through the ministry of the Holy Spirit, that 'other Paraclete' (helper, counsellor and comforter) whom he would send to them. And on the day of Pentecost they had had just this experience. Now their Master and Friend was spiritually available to each one of them, wherever they might happen to be, for he was omnipresent; and now, for the first time, it seemed natural and right to refer to him as the *Lord Jesus*.[23]

It was, indeed, this title, *Kyrios* or Lord, that soon became the most characteristic way of describing, or addressing, the risen Christ. That it was not confined to Gentile Christians, or even Hellenistic Jews, seems evident from the acclamation or prayer *Maranatha* ('Come, our Lord') preserved in its Aramaic form in 1 Corinthians 16:22. It was applied to Jesus in its full meaning, Oscar Cullmann insists, 'only after his death and exaltation',[24] and it implies not only allegiance and obedience, but worship. Its use in Hellenistic and Oriental mystery cults is sufficiently illustrated by St. Paul's statement in 1 Corinthians 8:5 and 6 that 'although there may be so-called gods in heaven or on earth – as indeed there are many "gods" and many "lords" – yet for us there is one God, the Father, from whom are all things and for whom we exist, and one Lord, Jesus Christ, through whom are all things and through whom we exist'. But its significance to Jews was even greater, for it was used in the Septuagint to translate the name of God (*Yahweh* or Jehovah) which the Jews hesitated even to pronounce, and for which they commonly substituted *Adonai* – which, Cullmann writes, 'was certainly the characteristic Jewish designation for God in the first century before and the first century after Christ'.[25] That the title should be instinctively – and without hesitation or ex-

---

[23] It will be found on analysis that the fairly frequent use of the word 'Lord' in regard to Jesus before the resurrection, particularly in the A. V., is almost always either in the vocative (where *kyrie* simply meant 'Sir') or in the *narrative* passages in Luke (where it must have come naturally to the author's pen).

[24] *The Christology of the New Testament*, p. 203. Cf. also Moule, *The Origin of Christology* pp. 35ff., and 148ff. for the use of this term.

[25] *Op. cit.* p. 200.

planation – used of the risen Christ by Jews who were monotheists through and through is, therefore, of profound significance. It is recorded, indeed, that even on the day of Pentecost St Peter declared that 'God has made him both Lord and Christ, this Jesus whom you crucified'.[26] Coupled with 'Jesus', this is presumably 'the name which is above every name' to which St. Paul refers in Philippians 2:9; for he immediately adds that 'at the name of Jesus every knee shall bow, in heaven and on earth and under the earth, and every tongue confess that Jesus Christ is *Lord,* to the glory of God the Father'. This constitutes irrefutable evidence that St. Paul – or, as many think, the words of a pre-Pauline Christian hymn which he quoted – did not hesitate to transfer to Jesus 'a great monotheistic passage from Isa. 45:23 in which God is represented as declaring that he must have no rivals'.[27] No wonder, then, that what seems to have been the earliest baptismal formula was the confession 'Jesus is Lord' – which equally signified that the Lord (with all that that title meant for a Jew) was identified with Jesus. It is clear, moreover, that from a very early date Christians felt perfectly free to address prayer specifically to the 'Lord Jesus'.[28] It is, indeed, often impossible to know whether a prayer which opens simply with the title 'Lord' is directed to the risen Christ or to God the Father; and it seems certain that the early Church made no sharp distinction in this respect. They were fully convinced that the Jesus who had been their teacher and master was now exalted to a place of supreme lordship or authority (for surely this is the sense in which the phrase 'at God's right hand' is to be understood?), and that one day he would come again in power as Lord of all. To suggest, therefore, that the Church 'must have allowed his memory gradually to be built up until it attained divine proportions', and the 'departed Master, at first merely invoked by his disciples, eventually becomes a cult deity, acclaimed by his worshippers', simply will not do. The evidence is dead against it.

[26] Acts 2:36.
[27] C. F. D. Moule, *op. cit.,* p. 41f.
[28] Cf. Acts 7:59.

If the deification of Jesus was the end result of an evolutionary process in pious imagination, how was it that a dedicated Jewish monotheist like Paul, at the earliest known stage of Christian literature, was already treating Christ as 'one with God'? Paul does not, it is true, use ontological terms of being or essence; but the implications of what he says are difficult to formulate without it. Whatever explanation is offered for this extraordinary phenomenon, the facile theory of an evolving superstition will not do. It simply does not fit the facts.[29]

How, then, did the apostolic Church now look back on the days of his earthly ministry; and how did they reconcile their view of the exalted Lord with the monotheism which was as precious to them as to the Judaism from which so many of them had sprung? One early answer to this question is provided by what is termed 'Adoptionism': namely, that Jesus was originally not only a true man (a fact which none of those who had 'companied' with him so intimately would have questioned for a moment), but nothing more than a man. Then, at a certain point, he was 'adopted' by God as his 'Son' and raised to divinity or quasi-divinity. Something like this, for example, was held soon after the fall of Jerusalem by Cerinthus (an Asian Jew who was an early Gnostic teacher), who believed that the purely human Jesus was chosen to be Son of God at his baptism when he was united with the aeon Christ – who was himself regarded as above the archangels but not fully divine. Different forms of 'adoptionism' have been expounded by a wide variety of teachers, some of them distinctly heretical and others rather more moderate, down the centuries. But should we be justified in concluding, with John Knox, that 'the earliest Christology was adoptionist' – as, he asserts, 'we should have expected it to be – but with the moment of adoption not his baptism, but rather his resurrection and exaltation'? The clearest example of this, in

[29] Moule, 'Incarnation: paradox that will not go away', in T.H.E.S., 23 Dec., 1977.

Knox's view, is Peter's statement, in Acts 2:36, that 'God has made this Jesus, whom you crucified, both Lord and Messiah', on which he comments: 'how can this passage be interpreted to mean anything else than that the man Jesus, crucified simply as such, was at the resurrection exalted to his present messianic status?' He admits that it can be clearly shown that

> the author of Luke-Acts had a higher or more advanced, a less simple Christology than the adoptionism I have described. The whole treatment of the earthly life of Jesus in the Gospel section of his work and many an allusion to it in the Acts section indicate beyond question that he did not think of Jesus' messiahship as having been conferred on him only after his human career had ended. Jesus was always 'Son of God'; he was not adopted or installed as such, whether at the resurrection or earlier.

But, he insists, the question 'is not whether the author of Luke-Acts held an adoptionist Christology but whether evidence for the primitive existence of such a Christology is to be found in his work'.[30]

It seems to me, however, that in this argument far too much emphasis is put on the single word 'made'. In a very similar passage St. Paul states that 'Jesus Christ our Lord' was 'descended from David according to the flesh and designated Son of God in power, according to the Spirit of holiness, by his resurrection from the dead.'[31] But this does not in any way imply that Jesus was not Son of God as well as son of David during his earthly ministry, but simply that he was openly shown and declared to be so by the resurrection. Again, Dr. John Robinson points out that there are many passages in the Epistle to the Hebrews which, taken by themselves, could well be interpreted in an adoptionist sense: for example, that Jesus was 'appointed the heir of all things', has 'become

[30] *The Humanity and Divinity of Christ* (C.U.P. 1967), pp. 7-9.
[31] Romans 1:3.

superior to the angels', was 'anointed with the oil of gladness above his fellows', was 'crowned with glory and honour because of the suffering of death', and was 'designated a high priest',[32] etc. But Robinson himself also calls attention to the fact that this same Epistle 'begins with the most stupendous affirmation of Christ, in contrast with all previous and partial revelations of God', as a Son 'who is the effulgence of God's splendour and the stamp of God's very being and sustains the universe by his word of power'.[33] Unless, therefore, we are to regard all the phrases in Hebrews which *could* be interpreted in an adoptionist sense as relics of an earlier view unconsciously preserved by the author – a suggestion which would, I think, stretch our credulity to the limit – it seems clear that the verses concerned should not be taken as evidence for any truly adoptionist Christology. This is brought into particularly sharp relief by the fact that the author couples in one sentence the statement that it was through the Son whom God '*appointed* heir of all things' that he had previously 'created the world'.[34] What these verses do emphasise, beyond question, is that whatever we are to think of Jesus during his earthly life – and, indeed, of the many New Testament references to his pre-existence, to which we must soon turn – there is a real sense in which the way in which he had been 'made like to his brethren', was 'in every respect tempted as we are', and, above all, had been willing to 'taste death for every one' and 'make propitiation for the sins of the people', had opened up what was clearly a new ministry as our High Priest 'in the power of an endless life'. Before he could assume this he *had,* indeed, to be 'made perfect through suffering' and to enter 'once for all into the Holy Place. . .through his own blood.'[35]

It is not only in the Epistle to the Hebrews, moreover, that we find references to the pre-existence of Christ. St. Paul, for example, refers to it – sometimes by direct statements and

[32] Heb. 1:2; 1:4; 1:9; 2:9; and 5:10.
[33] *The Human Face of God* (SCM Press, London, 1973), p. 155.
[34] Heb. 1:2.
[35] Cf. Heb. 2:17; 4:2; 9:2; 2:17; 7:16; 2:10; and 9:12.

sometimes by almost unconscious allusions – in a number of different contexts; and the fact that he does this without any argument or explanation demonstrates beyond doubt, as several authors have remarked, that the idea was widespread and well understood in the circles to which he was writing. This leads John Knox to admit that there are

> good reasons for believing that the Church's attribution of a divine pre-existence to Jesus was not, as it has sometimes been thought to be, the final step in a gradual process of pressing back the moment of his 'adoption' to an earlier and earlier time – from resurrection, to transfiguration, to baptism, to birth – until finally it was pushed out of the earthly life entirely and the idea of pre-existence was demanded. Such a process would have required time and could hardly have been completed early enough to account for the general acceptance of the idea in the period of Paul's letters. Rather, we are given grounds for believing – what would also seem inherently probable – that reflection on the resurrection and on the post-resurrection status of Christ led directly and immediately to the affirmation of his pre-existence.[36]

Much the same thesis has recently been discussed in far more detail by C. F. D. Moule in an article published in *Theologia Evangelica*[37], where he maintains that, although the New Testament writers differ considerably among themselves in their conceptions of how, precisely, the exalted Christ was – and is – experienced by Christians, 'they all seem unanimously to reflect two convictions: first, that the Lord whom they revere and acclaim is continuous with the Jesus of Nazareth who had been crucified: none other than Jesus himself; and secondly, that he is transcendent and divine.' So he asks the pertinent question: 'If, subsequently to

[36] *Op. cit.,* p. 11.
[37] Vol. VIII, No. 3, Sept., 1975.

his death, he is conceived of as an eternally living being, personal but more than individual, one with God and the source of salvation, and if he is still firmly identified with Jesus of Nazareth, then what of his pre-existence? Can "eternal" personality existing after the incarnation be denied existence before it?"[38]

Again, the conviction of Christ's pre-existence is at least as prominent in the Fourth Gospel as it is in the Pauline Epistles. Much has been written about the background to John's doctrine of the Logos in Stoic philosophy and, still more, in that of Philo of Alexandria, on the one hand, and in the Jewish belief in the 'Word of the Lord' by which the heavens were made (and which, like the Name of the Lord and the divine Wisdom, is almost personified in the Old Testament), on the other. But if, as is widely assumed, the Prologue to John's Gospel was written after the bulk of its contents, then it seems to me that we can scarcely doubt that a primary factor in the mind of the author must have been those allusions to pre-existence which he had already recorded as made by Jesus himself – however impossible it had been for the disciples to understand them at the time.[39] In what Dr. John Marsh aptly calls 'The Lord's Prayer' in chapter 17, for example, Jesus is recorded as having prayed: 'and now, Father, glorify thou me in thy own presence with the glory which I had with thee before the world was made.' On this R. H. Lightfoot remarks that 'The Lord. . .now prays that in this final hour He may be glorified at the Father's side with the glory which was His at the Father's side before the world existed', and comments: 'The glory for which the Lord, His work on earth completed, prays here, and to which He refers in 17:24, is the glory of the eternal Word, the glory which is His by nature and right;[40] and Marsh refers to the 'pre-

---

[38] Cf. also *The Origin of Christology*, pp. 136ff. *Pace* Dr. Young, *The Myth of God Incarnate*, pp. 21 and 35. But has anyone really suggested the 'simple equation: Jesus = God'. . . or that it is possible 'to reduce *all of God* to a human incarnation'?

[39] Even on the most critical view, these allusions must clearly be taken as evidence for the author's own conviction about the pre-existence of Jesus.

[40] *St. John's Gospel*, pp. 297ff.

mundial glory of the Son which was his before the world was made and historical time began'.[41]

This is not the place to embark on any discussion of the Logos doctrine, to which reference will frequently be made in this book. But in view of what I have just said it seems to me totally inadequate to interpret Christ's pre-existence, with several of those whose views we shall cite, simply in terms of fore-ordination, or of signifying that he had existed, before his human birth, only in the plan and mind of God. Knox tries to go marginally beyond this when he says that, when we join the Church

> in confessing the pre-existence, we are asserting. . .that God, the Father Almighty, Maker of the heavens and the earth, was back of, present in, and acting through the whole event of which the human life of Jesus was the centre. We are saying that *God* was in Christ – not in the resurrection only, but in the whole human career from conception through death. . .To say of the human Jesus, now exalted and transfigured, the 'first fruits' and the guarantor of humanity's redemption, that he had been in process of being created or begotten (in an organic view of reality this distinction loses much of its impor-tance) since time began, and that in God's 'mind' he existed 'before all worlds' – existed as the particular person he was and for the unique destiny he was to fulfil – to say this or something like this is to say all that can be said except in terms of myth or story.[42]

For in his view, to put the matter bluntly: 'We can have the humanity without the pre-existence and we can have the pre-existence without the humanity. There is absolutely no way of having both.'[43] But would not very much the same remark be equally applicable to any *full* belief in Christ's present

---

[41] St. John (The Pelican New Testament Commentaries, 1968), p. 559. At pp. 549-552 Marsh discusses the critical arguments relevant to John 17 as a whole.
[42] *Op. cit.,* pp. 107f.
[43] *Ibid.,* p. 106.

exaltation, as Professor Geoffrey Lampe recognises? What Knox, Robinson and a host of other contributors to what I have termed the 'contemporary debate' are determined at any cost to avoid is, of course, any form of Docetism – that is, the idea that Jesus was not really a man, in any full sense of that term, but a divine visitor who merely 'seemed' to be a man. This was, in fact, one of the very earliest heresies in the Church; and although it has been repeatedly repudiated and denied in our Creeds and formularies, there can be no doubt that what has been aptly termed 'psychological Docetism' has, all down the centuries, been an ever recurrent phenomenon. Indeed, as I look back at my own youth and early middle age, I am conscious that I thought of Jesus in such a way that his humanity was very largely swallowed up in his deity. In one sense this is, I think, almost inevitable, for we are now primarily concerned with the exalted Christ – quite apart from our view of his pre-existence, and of the doctrine of the Trinity as such. So, however much we may disagree with some of their conclusions, we owe a real debt to those of our contemporaries who have forced us to think much more radically and seriously of 'the *man* Christ Jesus', and to ponder anew the mystery of how the Word could, in very fact, '*become* flesh'.[44]

That, after all, is the fundamental problem of Christology – and it is immediately inherent in the simple confession: 'Jesus is Lord'. It is summed up, in a somewhat more theological form, in the doctrinal statement that he was, and is, 'Vere deus, vere homo' – truly God and truly man. But how can this be? How, in other words, can Christ be one with us, in our basic humanity, with all that this means, and yet one with God in his essential deity, with all that that implies? Both aspects of this problem are inevitably involved in the 'mystery of the Incarnation'. How could Godhead and humanity co-exist in one person – the Jesus of the Gospels? Was he a demigod, as the Arians used to assert, but as the Church firmly denied? Did he in fact have two natures – a human and a

---

[44] John 1:14.

divine – in one person, as classical orthodoxy declares? If so, were they strictly parallel, so that sometimes the one might be operative and sometimes the other, in a way which would appear almost schizophrenic? Or was the human nature somehow subsumed in the divine? All these points, and many others, were the subject of debate – and, indeed, bitter controversy – in past centuries of the Church's history. It was to guard against innumerable exaggerations, deviations and heresies that the Nicene Creed, the Definition of Chalcedon, and other doctrinal statements were drawn up. They have been much criticised, in the contemporary debate, because they are couched in a language which is not very meaningful today; because they are static rather than dynamic, ontological rather than functional; because they present us with a philosophical abstraction, rather than a living person; or because they go too far, whether positively or negatively, in trying to define the indefinable. Yet it is scarcely adequate, in terms of some devotional comments I have read, to remark: 'How a Person of the Godhead could become a babe, could join, in the most intimate union, His eternal wisdom with the innocence of a child; could unite infinite knowledge with a daily growth in knowledge; is beyond our comprehension. But it is so, and we can only bow and worship.' That we must 'bow and worship' I have no doubt whatever; but surely we must also make some attempt to understand, and to avoid making statements which seem merely to cancel one another out. It is partly, I think, the obscurantism in which we so often indulge in this context which has driven some contemporary theologians, as we shall see, to the verge of – or in some cases right into – Unitarianism.

What is not open to us, I suggest, is to dismiss the whole subject in the 'no nonsense' manner of C. Edward Barker, a Methodist minister turned psycho-therapist, in *The Church's Neurosis and Twentieth Century Revelations.* In this recent publication, commended in glowing terms by Canon J. Pearce-Higgins, the author writes of the Incarnation:

This doctrine is considered the foundation stone of

Christian belief. The incarnation affirms that the eternal God became man in the person of Jesus. In other words, Jesus was in fact God veiled in human flesh. As the author of Colossians wrote – 'For it is in Christ that the complete being of the Godhead dwells embodied'. This amazing statement implies that Jesus was not only divine by nature, was not only a Son of God, but was God himself in human form.

Then, after quoting part of the Nicene Creed and Paul Tillich's insistence that 'the assertion that "God has become man" is not a paradoxical but a nonsensical statement', Barker continues:

To attempt to tailor the concept of the incarnation to the needs of our scientific age, with its pragmatic and existential approach to life, is useless. These elaborate theological statements owe their origins, not to Jesus, but to the contentious theologians of the early Church. As for St. Paul, he was not concerned with the basic contents of Jesus' message. He was almost wholly obsessed with the idea of a 'cosmic catalyst', a divine intervener who would bring together Jews and gentiles into a harmony of belief, and would act as a salve for guilt.[45]

This summary repudiation, as 'patently unreasonable', 'nonsense', and 'no longer tenable', of a doctrine which has been accepted by the Church all down the centuries, treasured by its greatest saints and explored by its most brilliant thinkers, seems to me sheer arrogance – to say nothing of the positive parody of St. Paul's teaching. On such a basis there could, of course, be no such thing as an objective atonement, so it is natural enough that Barker should conclude that:

This 'reconciliation' by the cross – a cosmic event

[45] Rider, 1975, pp. 49ff.

whereby the 'Incarnate Son of God' bore the sins of the world in his own flesh – is not the good news of Jesus but an artifact of Paul. . .Paul's concentration on *the work of Christ* in dying for us on the cross has had the effect of turning Christianity into a morbid Crossianity. Paul's concentration on sin and its cleansing has led to obsessive traits in Christian believers. It has encouraged moral masochism, false piety and false humility, and not least, a pathetic 'Christian resignation' that is synonymous with defeatism.[46]

One turns with relief from such a complete caricature of both the New Testament and Christian experience to a writer like D. M. Baillie, who certainly cannot be accused of not taking the humanity of our Lord sufficiently seriously. Indeed, he goes so far as to suggest that

> God was continually pressing through into human life in every age, so far as man would allow, and the reason why the Incarnation did not take place earlier is because man was not sufficiently receptive. . . Therefore, when at last God broke through into human life with full revelation and became incarnate, must we not say that in a sense it was because here at last a Man was perfectly receptive?

But, however inadequate that statement may be, Baillie feels compelled to add:

> Yet there is more to be said. . . The divine is always prevenient. And so from the human life of Jesus on earth we are, paradoxically but inevitably, led back to its divine origin and eternal background in heaven, on which it all depended. 'When the fullness of time was come, God sent forth his Son', and He who was 'born of a woman, born under the law', lived as He did because He was Son of God.[47]

[46] *Ibid.,* pp. 54f.
[47] *God was in Christ* (Faber and Faber, London, 1961 edition), pp. 149f.

2
Christology Down the Centuries

IN MY FIRST CHAPTER I TRIED TO ETCH IN SOME OF THE background to the contemporary debate about the Incarnation and to outline part of the New Testament data. In subsequent chapters, moreover, we shall be concerned with the current controversy in much more detail – first against the backcloth of other religions, and then in terms of a detailed consideration of the views of a few representative scholars – before attempting to draw the subject together and come to some tentative conclusions. But at this point it would, I think, be useful – particularly for those who have a minimal, or somewhat rusty, knowledge of the history of Christian doctrine – to interpose a synopsis of the way in which christological thought has developed down the centuries, and the constant recurrence, in many different forms, of some of the basic problems with which we are still grappling today and to which further references must inevitably be made.

Some readers may, however, find this summary of the controversies of the past too detailed and technical for their taste, and prefer to concentrate exclusively on the contemporary situation. For such it may suffice to say that the classical formulas in which the historic faith of the Church has been expressed – such as the 'Nicene Creed', the 'Definition of Chalcedon', etc. – were the result of the need to express and safeguard, against a number of views which were felt to be deviant or erroneous, two basic truths: first, that Jesus was both God and man; secondly, that he was one person, not two. Even on this basis there were, of course, different ways in which the 'Mystery of the Incarnation' could be approached and understood; and it is fascinating to note

34

how constantly theories which seem to be new represent little more than a restatement, perhaps with minor variations, of some thesis which has been debated and discarded long ago, or even repeatedly. The purpose of this chapter is to sum- marise, for those who want this, the way in which these formulas were evolved and debated (usually in the course of controversy, and in a form which was dictated, in part, by the philosophical thought-patterns of the day) from the primary testimony of the New Testament and the living experience of the Church. But it would be perfectly possible for some readers to skim or even skip this chapter – for the present at least.

We have seen how the disciples regarded Jesus, during the days of his ministry, as teacher, prophet and Messiah – but unquestionably as a man among men. So the crucifixion must have shattered all their hopes, for how could one who had been condemned and executed as a criminal be the promised Redeemer of Israel? Instead of being vindicated by God he had, to all appearances, been rejected by him; and it was only the cataclysmic experience of the resurrection which brought them, bewildered and at first doubting, to a wondering and unquenchable joy. Now they were convinced that the 'Lord' Jesus had been 'exalted to the right hand of God' and would one day come again to usher in the Kingdom he had preached. Instinctively, therefore, they began to associate him with God, and sometimes to address him in prayer. At an ex- ceedingly early date, moreover, they came to believe in his pre-existence, in the role he had played in the very creation of the world, and in the fact that all things that exist are 'held together in him' – for it is deeply significant that none of the attacks on St. Paul and his teaching during his lifetime seem to have been directed against his Christology.

It is scarcely surprising, therefore, that one of the earliest Christian heresies, to which references are made in the New Testament itself, was what came to be known as Docetism; for it was natural enough that Gentile converts, who had never known 'the man, Christ Jesus', should sometimes think of him in terms of a theophany. In its extreme form Docetism was the belief that Jesus had never, in fact, been a man at all; he had, indeed, *seemed* to be a man, but he was really God – or at least a divine being – appearing in human guise. That some such view was propagated by false teachers at a very early date is amply attested by the Johannine Epistles. The first letter propounds two basic tests of whether any doctrine is inspired by the 'Spirit of God' or the spirit of 'Anti-Christ'. One of these is whether the doctrine concerned affirms or denies that 'Jesus Christ has come in the flesh'[1] – a criterion which is also enunciated in the statement in the second letter that 'many deceivers have gone out into the world, men who will not acknowledge the coming of Jesus Christ in the flesh; such a one is the deceiver and the anti-Christ'.[2] And in less extreme forms, which do not deny that Jesus had a genuinely human body – or even both body and psyche – but which, in one way or another, deny his full and complete manhood, Docetism (or 'psychological Docetism') has been an ever-recurrent phenomenon which has never ceased to trouble the Church.

The other criterion of false teaching in 1 John is whether it so fails to confess that 'Jesus is the Christ' that it in fact denies 'the Father and the Son'.[3] This test was, presumably, primarily aimed at Jewish-Christian 'Ebionites' who regarded Jesus as the Messiah, and in some sense even as a transcendent being, but denied that he was Son of God, virgin-born or pre-existent.[4] It would also cover Gnostic sectaries who, like the followers of Cerinthus, regarded Jesus as having been a mere man until he was united, at his baptism, with the aeon Christ – who left him, according to one form of this teaching, before the passion.[5] It was against such perversions of the truth that the explicit reference to Jesus as 'the Son of God. . .who came with water and blood' ('not by water only,

---

[1] 1 John 4:2f.
[2] 2 John 7.
[3] 1 John 2:22.
[4] Aloys Grillmeier, *Christ in Christian Tradition* (trans. by John Bowden, Mowbrays, London, 1965; revised edition 1975), pp. 76f.
[5] G. L. Carey, *The New International Dictionary of the Christian Church* (British ed., The Paternoster Press, Exeter, 1974), p. 207.

but by water and blood')[6] was directed, according to the interpretation of this somewhat obscure allusion first suggested by Tertullian: namely, that the 'water' refers to his baptism, at which the divine voice proclaimed him to be 'My beloved Son', while the 'blood' represents a sort of shorthand symbol for his death on the cross. As in the case of Docetism, this extreme form of Gnostic teaching has long since disappeared. But somewhat similar, although more moderate, doctrines, which may be grouped together under the umbrella of Adoptionism, have reappeared, as we have seen, down the centuries – some more, and some less, heretical – and are often claimed to be the earliest form of Christology.

It was, of course, inevitable that the confession that 'Jesus is Lord' should raise theological problems. The *kerygma* not only proclaimed the risen Christ as exalted to God's right hand, but explicitly identified him with Jesus of Nazareth; and this was bound to give rise, sooner rather than later, to christological debate. But the major problem of the second and third centuries revolved round the nature of God. This was natural enough, for the unity of the Godhead was fundamental to Judaism. How, then, could Jewish Christians call Jesus Lord, address him in prayer, and somehow identify him with Yahweh? Had they ceased to be monotheists? Or did this mean that there was a previously unsuspected complexity in the divine unity which went far beyond the semi-personification of Wisdom, and the Spirit and Word of the Lord, in the Old Testament? This problem was first apprehended, it seems, in 'binitarian' terms, which concentrated only on the Father and the Son; but later it came to take a trinitarian form.

But how, in either case, was the differentiation within the unity of the Godhead to be understood? Was it in terms of what came to be called 'Monarchianism' – a name derived from the Greek word *monarchia* which emphasises 'the sole rule of God or one sole originating principle in God', but

---

[6] 1 John 5:5 and 6.

which was in fact used in reference to two distinct schools of thought? The first, properly known as 'Dynamic Monarchianism', seems to represent a dubious use of the term, for it was applied to men who 'affirmed two entities in the Godhead (the Father and the Son or the Spirit) without any special emphasis either on the unity of the Godhead or on their relation to each other'. They were called Dynamic Monarchians because they held that the divine rested upon the man Jesus as a power *(dynamis)*; so their teaching could aptly be described as 'Dynamic Binitarianism'. The other heresy was that of 'Modalist Monarchianism', a term applied to those who understood the distinctions in the Godhead as no more than three 'modes' or manifestations of the divine unity. Early Modalists, like Dynamic Monarchians, phrased their doctrine purely in terms of the Father and the Son; but on their premises, as Professor H. E. W. Turner observes, 'three modes would present no more difficulty than two'. It was in fact in a trinitarian form that Sabellius expounded Modalism early in the third century; and the essence of his teaching was that God is by nature a monad, one *hypostasis* or essence with three names or modes of revelation, which Sabellius apparently regarded as successive rather than simultaneous.[7] Praxeas, another Modalist, 'exaggerated the idea of the monarchy', and (to quote Aloys Grillmeier)

> sought to bring his trinitarian modalism into his teaching on the incarnation as well, and to interpret Christ as a manifestation of the Father. On the one hand he wants to say that the Father became man and suffered (hence the name patripassianism), but on the other he must concede that scripture ascribes the Incarnation to a 'Son'. So as not to have to give up his ideas of the exaggerated *monarchia,* he helps himself by describing the 'flesh' as the new subject to which the title of Son pertains. Then the relationship between Father and Son described in the scriptures is only an apparent

[7] Cf. H. E. W. Turner, in *A Dictionary of Christian Theology* (ed. by Alan Richardson, SCM Press, 1969), pp. 223, 220f., and 299.

relationship which knows no real difference of the persons. The 'flesh' and the *spiritus,* which is the Father, i.e. the unipersonal God of Praxeas, together make up the Christ of patripassianism; a very rare christological framework *spiritus-caro*.[8]

Tertullian, who denounced this teaching, was 'himself a defender of the *monarchia*', but in the much more orthodox form of what came to be termed the 'Economic Trinity'. Economic Trinitarianism held that the Son and the Spirit did not 'have the status of full *Hypostases* but of economies or functional dispensations of the one God extrapolated for the purposes of creation and redemption'.[9] Tertullian's own view, for most of his life, was that

> Father, Son and Spirit are in the one total reality of God. The Son proceeds from this one *substantia* as it is in the Father and thereby receives his own reality, without being separated. Son and Spirit are distinguished through the order of their origin. Tertullian also describes the character of the Son (and the Spirit) by the word *portio*. This does not mean 'part' *(pars)*. The Son is not a 'part' of the divine substance, but has a 'share' in it. . . The divine substance is essentially one; the Son is, as it were, an effluence of this one substance. . .'[10]

But Economic Trinitarianism reached its most sophisticated form in Marcellus of Ancyra, 'with precisely dated extrapolations and the return of the Godhead into monadic isolation at the conclusion of the economy'.[11] It has, moreover, been espoused in a very modified form, in recent years, by Karl Barth among others, largely because of the misunderstanding to which the use of the term 'Persons' in relation to the Godhead may so easily give rise today. Barth

---

[8] Grillmeier, *op. cit.,* p. 121 – largely based on Tertullian *Against Praxeas*.
[9] Turner, pp. 334 and 345.
[10] Cf. Grillmeier, *op. cit.,* p. 119.
[11] Turner, *op. cit.,* p. 345.

prefers, therefore, to speak of three 'modes of being' in God. But this is not Modalism in the heretical or Sabellian sense, which Barth regards as a grave error. His concept of the doctrine of the Trinity stands for

> real distinctions in God, and, moreover, for the kind of distinctions on which orthodox belief has always insisted: the three Persons are not *parts* of God, and yet they are not mere attributes, relative to our apprehension. . .but are of the eternal being of the God who has revealed Himself to us in Christ and dwells in us by the Holy Spirit.[12]

The opposite pole from Modalism, or from any monist theory of the nature of God, is that of Tritheism, 'in which the plurality of the persons approximates to belief in three Gods' (of which, at a later date, the Cappadocean Fathers were mistakenly accused). In its extreme form this opened the door, as it were, to the Arian heresy, which included in a single formula a Father who was fully God, a Son who had the status of a leading creature and a Spirit who was inferior to the Son.[13] In general terms, however, the West can be said to have adopted, from Tertullian to Augustine, a firmly monist starting point in their approach to the doctrine of the Trinity, while in the East 'pluralism based on a Platonic interpretation of Christianity became the dominant tradition'.[14] This was developed by Origen, whose trinitarian doctrine was pluralist in framework, and whose special contribution was the doctrine of the eternal generation of the Son by the Father. But although, in his view, all the members of the Trinity were divine, this was, it seems, in a 'graded Trinity' in which the Son mediated the Father to the created world and the Spirit was the first production of the Son.[15]

---

[12] Cf. D. M. Baillie, *op. cit.,* pp. 135ff.

[13] Cf. Turner, *op. cit.,* p. 351.

[14] *Ibid.,* p. 346.

[15] Cf. R. P. C. Hanson, in *A Dictionary of Christian Theology,* p. 245. But it should be noted, in this context, that Origen also believed in the eternal creation of the world (or, perhaps, in a succession of worlds) by the eternally-generated Logos.

From what I have already said two points, I think, stand out clearly. First, it was the resurrection, and the consequent conviction that the exalted Lord was somehow one with the Father, that forced the early Church to ponder the nature of the Godhead. It is only natural, therefore, that they often spoke in binitarian terms, and that a full trinitarian doctrine should come later. But a strong case can be made for the claim that this was not 'a sort of evolutionary process' but merely a development of what was already inherent, if not explicit, in the New Testament.[16] Secondly, two approaches to the differentiations within the Godhead were possible.

> Monist theologians started from the unity of the Godhead and worked tentatively towards divine plurality. . . Pluralist thinkers, on the other hand, maintained the full co-presence of two (later three) distinct entities within the Godhead and sought a bond of unity strong enough to support their convictions. Unity of derivation from the Father (the Monarchy), harmony of will and finally identity of substance, *Ousia (Homoousios)*, were all laid under contribution.[17]

This digression into some of the developments in trinitarian doctrine during the second and third centuries helps to explain why the great christological controversies of the fourth and fifth centuries tended at first to concentrate on the divine rather than the human problems inherent in the doctrine of the Incarnation, and took what may be termed the downward rather than the upward approach. But the 'Apologists' of the second and third centuries, such as Justin Martyr and Athenagoras, had in a sense paved the way for later controversies by the way in which they tried to express their understanding of the faith in the philosophical language

---

[16] For the difference between 'evolution' and 'development' in Christology, see C. F. D. Moule, *The Origin of Christology*, pp. 1-3; for the 'development' of the doctrine of the Trinity, see Arthur W. Wainwright, *The Trinity in the New Testament* (SPCK, London, 1962), *passim*.

[17] Turner, *op. cit.*, p. 345.

of their educated contemporaries. In this task they relied greatly on the concept of the Logos, or 'Word' of God. The contemporary view of God in Hellenistic thought was so abstract and transcendent that he could have no contact with the world except through a mediator; and this function only the Logos could perform. To the Apologists he was a product of the Father's will. Although eternally immanent as a principle in God, in due time he came forth in order to create all things. 'Finite in His own being, since there was a time when He began to be, He forms the natural organ of revelation to the finite', and though 'subordinate to the highest God,' he might 'be called a second God, and ought to be worshipped.'[18]

The Apologists were followed by Irenaeus, Tertullian, Clement and Origen, who all put a major emphasis on the divine Logos. Irenaeus taught that, as Logos, God had always been manifested in the world, first through the prophets, and finally in Christ his Son. 'Through the Word Himself, who had become visible and palpable', he affirmed, 'was the Father shown forth; all saw the Father in the Son: for the Father is the invisible of the Son, but the Son the visible of the Father.' So Irenaeus tended 'to construe the Logos not as somehow a portion of the Godhead, much less a second, inferior God, but as God himself breaking forth in revelation' – a view which clearly prepared the way for the Modalist Monarchianism to which reference has already been made. To Tertullian (who was, it seems, the first person to use the word *trinitas* and to construct the formula 'One substance, three persons') the Logos was first 'existent in God, as it were. . .in potentiality', and then 'arose out of God as Son by generation before all worlds, being thus projected, or invested with independent being, with a view to the creation of the universe. Thus He had a beginning'. And it was this pre-existent Logos or Son who, in the fullness of time, assumed flesh for our salvation – which represents 'the last

[18] H. R. Mackintosh, *The Doctrine of the Person of Christ* (T. and T. Clark, Edinburgh, 1912), p. 141.

stage in the coming of the Logos to full personal existence'. Clement in turn, concentrated on the Logos doctrine in a way which tended, partially, to 'depersonalise the historic Saviour'. Viewed from below, as Mackintosh puts it, 'He appears as the fullness of the Godhead, concentrated in an independent life; from above He is the highest next to the Almighty, the minister of God, mediating all created life, and at a certain distance from the Father as the absolute monad'. But Clement could be strangely self-contradictory. Origen, as we have seen, insisted that, as Son, the Logos proceeds from the Father by an eternal generation. Hence to say that a time was when the Son was not, was an error.[19]

By contrast, Arius flatly asserted that, if the Father 'begat' the Son, there *must* have been a time when the Son did not exist. God was a remote and inaccessible Being who did not himself create the world except, indirectly, through the Logos, who was at one and the same time a divine and a created being. This was no mere matter of theological hair-splitting, as D. M. Baillie emphasises, nor was it

> an argument as to whether there was in Jesus a super-natural incarnation of the heavenly pre-existent Logos or Son of God, for the Arians themselves believed that the Logos or Son of God, who had existed from before all ages in glory as a heavenly being above all angels, had come to earth through a virgin birth, lived a super-natural life in a human body, was crucified, rose from the dead, and ascended to heaven, to be worshipped with divine honours. They believed all that. But what availed all that, when they did not believe that this Logos was of one essence with God the Father?

For on this basis 'it is not the eternal God himself that comes to us in Christ for our salvation, but an intermediate being, distinct from God, while God himself is left out, uncondescending, unredemptive.'[20]

[19] Cf. Mackintosh, *op. cit.*, pp. 145; 334 and 154ff.; 162f.; and 165; but see also pp. 40 and 42 above.
[20] D. M. Baillie, *op. cit.*, p. 70.

But this doctrine was just as destructive in the realm of Christology as in that of the Trinity, for the Arians regarded the Son as a sort of demi-god; 'a creature, but not as one of the creatures'. He was a mediator between God and man by being himself neither fully God nor fully man, rather than by being both at one and the same time. They supported their case by pointing to the Gospels, which make it perfectly clear that Jesus grew in wisdom, did not know the date of his Second Advent, and suffered not only in body but also in soul. They attributed all this, moreover, to the divine Logos incarnate in him; so this meant that the Logos could change, could be ignorant and could suffer. But God – in the dominant philosophical view of the day – was not only transcendent and self-existent, but also immutable, omniscient and impassible. Clearly, then, the Logos could not be fully God. The Arians, moreover, do not seem to have been greatly concerned with the doctrine of redemption; so Turner remarks that 'an important control on their Christology was missing', and that Arianism was as defective in its view of the work of Christ as of his person.[21] But the Arian heresy was denounced at the Council of Nicaea in 325 A.D., which promulgated the Nicene Creed.[22] This includes the words:

> We believe. . .in one Lord Jesus Christ, the Son of God, begotten from the Father, only-begotten, that is, from the substance of the Father, God from God, light from light, true God from true God, begotten not made, of one substance with the Father, through whom all things came into being, things in heaven and things on earth, who because of us men and because of our salvation came down and became incarnate, becoming man. . .[23]

[21] H. E. W. Turner, *Jesus the Christ* (Mowbrays, London, 1976), pp. 32ff.

[22] Which differs from the 'Nicene Creed' recited in the Communion service in the Church of England. This is often called the 'Niceno-Constantinopolitan Creed', in the belief that it was promulgated by the Council of Constantinople in A.D. 381. But this is doubtful.

[23] Grillmeier, *op. cit.*, p. 267.

It is noteworthy that Christ is designated 'Son', rather than Logos; that the two phrases 'the first-born of all creation' and 'begotten of the Father before all ages' (both of which the Arians would have affirmed) were omitted; that 'begotten, not made' and the crucial 'of one substance with the Father' were inserted; and that the addition of 'was made man' to 'was made flesh' ruled out the Arian belief that Jesus had a human body but not a human soul.[24]

Athanasius, the leading opponent of Arius, did not become a bishop until a year after the Council, although he seems to have played a considerable part in it. His principal emphasis – in sharp contrast to the Arians – was on the doctrine of salvation. Man had sinned, and in consequence had become both corrupt and mortal. Repentance alone would not save him; God himself must intervene. So Athanasius insisted that the Son was not merely 'like' the Father, but 'the same in likeness'; that 'He did not receive in reward the name of the Son and God, but rather He Himself has made us sons of the Father, and deified men by becoming Himself man'. Indeed, 'the same things are said of the Son which are said of the Father, except His being said to be Father.' Arius, he said, taught pure polytheism; 'for if the Father is not Father everlastingly, and if in time a Son emerges, as the finite progeny of Godhead, and afterwards a Spirit lower still, who can answer for it that this is the end?'[25]

The Council of Nicaea, then, affirmed unequivocally that the divine Son, incarnate in Jesus, was one in essence with the Father. It had also been assumed from the first that he was truly man; and this had been firmly asserted in opposition to Gnostic Docetism. But how were the divine and human united in one person? What was the bond between them, and what emphasis should be given to each? On this a certain division of opinion had begun to appear even before the Arian controversy, and two traditions continued to exist after the Council. Neither tradition, Turner insists, was unorthodox in itself, though both 'were liable to produce

[24] Cf. Mackintosh, *op. cit.,* pp. 181f.
[25] Cf. Mackintosh, *op. cit.,* pp. 183ff.

equal and opposite exaggerations which were condemned as heretical'. Both, moreover, 'worked within a common framework of the doctrine of God as absolute, impassible and immutable', and both were firmly orthodox in their doctrine of the Trinity. But one tradition, mainly associated with Alexandria, was 'Monist' in tendency, and the other, linked with the Patriarchate of Antioch, was Dualist in inclination. The first has been described as the 'Word-flesh' tradition, with its Christology, in Turner's words,

> firmly anchored in the Godhead both as its starting-point and as the organising principle within the incarnate Person. The Logos was the ultimate subject even of the incarnate experience of Christ. . . The emphasis lay upon the unity of the Person of Christ and the description of the tradition as Monist may therefore be equally apt. The Incarnation involved a divine descent into human life or, as Prestige describes it, a divine irruption or inbreaking. Its favourite proof-text was John 1:14; and, though it could recognise that 'flesh' was a piece of biblical shorthand for 'man', it tended to regard the humanity as adjectival or instrumental to the divinity. . . Its doctrine of Redemption was equally centred in God. If the work of Christ was to avail for all men and be transmissible to all it must be centrally and vitally an act of God. In expositions of the doctrine of vicarious victory it is always the divine Logos who is the mighty victor on behalf of men.[26]

By contrast, the second tradition has been called the 'Word-man' tradition;

> but since it emphasised the full co-presence of two simultaneous natures, Godhead and manhood, the label of Dualist may be equally appropriate. While not denying the involvement of God the Logos in the incarnate life it was chiefly concerned to provide

[26] Turner, *Jesus the Christ*, p. 37.

adequate living space for the humanity of Christ which was more highly valued and more realistically conceived than in the rival tradition. . . The Incarnation then involved not a substantial union of the Logos with the flesh but a looser conjunction of the divine Logos with a complete humanity. . . Its favourite proof-text was Phil. 2:5-11, where 'being in the form of God' (verse 6) and 'taking the form of a servant' (verse 7) were taken as references to two simultaneous co-present natures within the incarnate Lord. . . In their doctrine of Redemption they assigned a real and sometimes a predominant place to the humanity of Christ.[27]

The Monist tradition, in its most extreme form, gave rise to the 'Apollinarian heresy', named after Apollinarius of Laodicea (d. 390 c.). This is often regarded as a reaction against Arianism; but Grillmeier insists that *logically* Christology 'might well have made the transition from Apollinarianism to Arianism, but not vice versa', since the latter

is no more than a development of the basic principles of the former. The 'Apollinarian' view of the physical, vital conjunction of Logos and sarx already contains the germ of that vitiation of the transcendence of the Logos which Arianism developed consistently. The strict Logos-sarx framework, which makes the Logos the soul, necessarily tends towards the Arian devaluation of the Logos. . .[28]

In the Nicene Creed the words 'was made man' had been added to 'made flesh' to combat Arian doctrines; but, in spite of this, some degree of Docetism was at that time widespread. 'If perfect God were joined to perfect man, they would be two', Apollinarius argued, and a man-God is unthinkable. So at first he denied the entirety of Christ's

---

27 *Ibid.*, pp. 37ff.
28 Grillmeier. *op. cit.*, p. 330. But chronologically, of course, Arianism preceded Apollinarianism.

human nature, acknowledging only that he had a human body; but later he affirmed that his *psyche,* too, was human, but that the place of his human 'spirit' or mind *(pneuma* or *nous)* was taken by the Logos. The result was a 'living unity' in which, he said, there was 'only one activity, one nature *(physis),* one *hypostasis,* one *prosōpon'* – although it is far from clear what distinction he made between these terms. 'But whatever else of humanity Apollinarius believed the Logos to have assumed, Turner emphasises, the *nous* or directive principle was lacking'; and this was vital, since Apollinarius regarded the *nous,* not the body, as the seat of sin.[29] It was in regard to this very truncated (and hopelessly inadequate) view of the Incarnation that Gregory of Nazianzus made his famous remark that 'What he did not assume, he did not heal [or redeem]'.

The most extreme form of the Dualist (or Antiochene) school of thought is represented by the 'Nestorian heresy', which derived its name from Nestorius (d. 451 c.), although Theodore of Mopsuestia had in fact led the way. For Theodore the integrity of Christ's humanity was just as important as the transcendence of the divine Logos, for it was 'as man that Christ triumphed over sin and death and therefore for redemptive as well as christological reasons he must have both a human soul and will'. In his teaching a clear distinction is drawn between the two natures. After the Virgin Birth there was a 'conjunction' *(sunapheia)* of these two natures, and the divine 'indwelt' the human by God's 'good pleasure' *(eudokia).* He uses the terms *physis, hypostasis* and *prosōpon;* but, while he clearly accepted two natures, Turner says that it is probable that he affirmed one *prosōpon,* and 'wholly uncertain whether he wrote of one or two *hypostases.'*[30]

---

[29] Cf. Mackintosh, *op. cit.,* pp. 198f.; Turner, in *A Dictionary of Christian Doctrine,* p. 56 and *Jesus the Christ,* p. 40. Cf. also Baillie, *op. cit.,* p. 88; G. T. D. Angel, in *The New International Dictionary of the Christian Church,* p. 56; and Grillmeier, *op. cit.,* pp. 330ff.

[30] Cf. Turner, *Jesus the Christ,* pp. 47ff.; *A Dictionary of Christian Doctrine,* p. 57.

A clash between the two schools was not long delayed. The protagonists were Cyril of Alexandria (d. 444 c.) and Nestorius, and the occasion was Nestorius' objection to Cyril's use of the term 'Mother of God' of the Virgin Mary. This term was common coin at Alexandria, but somewhat suspect among the Antiochenes, who maintained that 'God the Word' should be sharply distinguished from the man Jesus, who was not deified but 'taken into a unique personal conjunction with the Logos, and after the resurrection lifted up to a share in his universal power'. Another point of difference between the two traditions was 'the christological technique known as *communicatio idiomatum* whereby attributes or activities proper to one nature are seemingly attributed to the other because of the unity of Person which includes or possesses both.[31]

Nestorius uses the terms *ousia* (substance), *physis* (nature) and *prosōpon* (external appearance) in his analysis of a concrete person, and sometimes uses the term *hypostasis* as well, but with a meaning which seems to vary according to the context.[32] His chief opponent, Cyril, followed Apollinarius in describing the Incarnation of the Logos as *kenōsis* ('condescension'); or, in his own words, *krypsis* ('veiling') of the glory of the Logos to make it bearable for men. It also implied *prolepsis* (addition) in the sense of assuming the 'limiting conditions of humanity'. Cyril's major interest, like that of Athanasius, was the doctrine of redemption: humanity imbued with deity through the Incarnation. So he insisted that 'if the Word did not suffer for us humanly, He did not accomplish our redemption divinely; if He who suffered for us was mere man and but the organ of deity, we are not in fact redeemed'.[33] The Logos not only assumed, but became, flesh. For Cyril, Christ's human nature was 'impersonal' *(anhypostatos)*, since his human nature was 'personal only in the Logos'; and 'as soul and body are one in us, so

[31] Turner, *Jesus the Christ,* pp. 48f.; Mackintosh, *op. cit.,* p. 204.
[32] Turner, *op. cit.,* pp. 49f.
[33] Cf. Turner, *op. cit.,* pp. 43f.; Mackintosh, *op. cit.,* p. 207.

Godhead and manhood were made the one Christ'. Of the passion Cyril affirmed that 'the impassible Logos suffered in the passible flesh' – or even that 'he suffered impassibly'; while in regard to his apparent ignorance he commented: 'He usefully pretended not to know'.[34]

The dispute between Cyril and Nestorius resulted in the deposition of both of them by the supporters of the other faction at Ephesus in 431 A.D., although the decision in regard to Cyril was soon reversed. When Cyril died in 444 A.D., however, his central thesis was espoused by Eutyches, who was considerably more extreme, but eventually contented himself with affirming: 'I confess our Lord to have become out of two natures before the union. But I confess one nature after the union'. A new Council, described by Leo of Rome as the 'Robber Council', was called at Ephesus in 449 A.D., to which Leo sent his 'Dogmatic Epistle'; but it was not until two years later, at the Council of Chalcedon, in 451 A.D., that both Eutychianism and Nestorianism were condemned as heretical. This Council primarily 'sought to discover the solution to just *one* disputed question: *how* the confession of the *'one Christ'* may be reconciled with belief in the *'true God and true man'*, *'perfect in Godhead, perfect in manhood'*.[35] Eventually, the assembled Fathers promulgated their famous Definition. This began by confessing the Church's belief that 'our Lord Jesus Christ is one and the same Son' – a simple formula in which Alexandrians and Antiochenes could meet[36] – and then continued:

> The Same perfect in Godhead, the Same perfect in manhood, truly God and truly man, the Same [consisting] of a rational soul and a body; *homoousios*[37] with the Father as to his Godhead, and the Same *homoousios* with us as to his manhood; in all things like unto us, sin only excepted; begotten of the Father

[34] Mackintosh, *op. cit.*, pp. 205f.; Turner, *op. cit.*, pp. 44f.
[35] Grillmeier, *op. cit.*, pp. 544f.
[36] *Ibid.*, p. 546.
[37] i.e. 'consubstantial'.

before ages as to his Godhead, and in the last days, the Same, for us and for our salvation, of Mary the Virgin *Theotokos* as to his manhood.

On this part of the Definition Grillmeier comments:

> Motifs recur from an earlier period, the time of the struggle against Gnostics and docetists. The Arian and Apollinarian denial of the completeness of Christ's human nature is also refuted: Christ has a rational soul and a truly human body. Nothing may be taken away from the human nature of Christ to explain his unity. . . [A] chief concern, however, is to express both the distinction and the completeness of Godhead and manhood. To do this, the most disputed word of the fourth century, the *homoousion,* is recalled this time to be used of both the Godhead and the manhood.[38]

But *how* was both the unity and the distinction of Godhead and manhood in Christ to be understood? At this point the Definition – which could be said to have approximated to the views of Cyril in many respects – in one critical point bowed to the moderating influence of Leo and the Western Church,[39] for it continued:

> . . .acknowledged in two natures without confusion, without change, without division, without separation – the difference of the natures being by no means taken away because of the union, and [each] combining in one Person and *hypostasis* – not divided or separated into two Persons, but one and the same Son and only-begotten God, Word, Lord Jesus Christ. . .[40]

[38] *Op. cit.,* p. 547.
[39] Cf. Mackintosh, *op. cit.,* p. 213; Turner, *Jesus the Christ,* pp. 54f. who notes that the phrase 'truly God and truly man' was 'a characteristically Dualist expression'.
[40] Translation according to E. R. Hardy, ed. *Christology of the Later Fathers* (1954), p. 573.

On this Turner comments:

> While the paragraph is primarily concerned with the duality of the natures it opens and ends with a strong affirmation of unity. The four negative adverbs are paired off against Monist and Dualist exaggerations. 'Without confusion' is aimed at the use by Eutyches of mixture language; 'without change' directed against Arianism. 'Without division, without separation' excludes Nestorius as currently interpreted.[41]

But the Definition, naturally enough, did not satisfy either the Nestorians or the Monophysites. The Nestorians disliked it because in their eyes a hypostatic or personal union was virtually equivalent to a natural union (that is, one in which 'the ground or possibility of unification lay in the natures themselves'), and the Monophysites (who called those who believed in the two natures in the one person of Christ Dyophysites) disliked it because to them a hypostatic or personal union was no substitute for a natural one;[42] and they argued that 'all that is divine in Christ is also human, and all that is human is also divine'. But it may also be criticised as providing – inevitably, no doubt, at that time – a largely abstract, philosophical definition which seems not only negative but strangely remote from the Jesus of the Gospels.

Basic to this definition, in John McIntyre's view,[43] is Aristotelian logic, for it was fundamental to Aristotle's system to make a sharp distinction between 'primary substance' and 'secondary substance'. The examples of 'primary substance' he gives are an individual man or horse. Of these a number of 'secondary substances' can be predicated, such as that both the man and the horse belong to the genus

[41] *Jesus the Christ*, p. 55.
[42] Cf. Turner, in *A Dictionary of Christian Theology*, p. 58.
[43] *The Shape of Christology* (SCM Press, 1966), pp. 82-100. But cf., in this context, C. Stead, *Divine Substance* (Clarendon Press, Oxford, 1977), especially pp. 113ff.

'animal', and that the man also belongs to the species 'human'. Equally, of course, it may be said that the man or the horse is the subject of suitable 'circumstances, characteristics, qualities and experiences'. But it is impossible to 'predicate' a particular man or horse of, or to say that he 'exists' in, anything or anyone else. Secondary substances, on the other hand, can only exist in, or be predicated of, something else: i.e. some primary substance.

When applied to Christology this meant that neither the divine nor the human nature *(physis)* could exist without a *hypostasis.* This is a word which some writers had identified with *ousia* (substance or essence), some with *physis* (nature) and some even with *prosōpon* (person, or outward appearance), and it is exceedingly difficult to translate. When applied to the Trinity it came to be used of the personal distinctions which exist within the one substance or essence of the Godhead; and when applied to Christ it came to be used in the sense that a *physis* (nature), whether human or divine, cannot exist without a *hypostasis* (entity) to which it belongs or adheres: 'no *physis* without a *hypostasis*'; or 'no *physis anhypostatos.*'

This principle was apparently ignored in the Definition of Chalcedon, McIntyre insists, for this affirms the existence of two natures, without confusion and without change, in one person *(prosopon)* and *hypostasis.* It is preserved, of course, although in very different ways, in Nestorianism, which assigns to the one person both two natures and two *hypostases,* and in Eutychianism, which acknowledges only one nature in Christ 'after the union'. But it is also preserved in the formula by which Leontius of Jerusalem[44] suggested that, instead of leaving the human nature of our Lord without a *hypostasis* (a *physis anhypostatos*), as in the Definition, it should be regarded as having no *hypostasis* of its own, but finding its *hypostasis* in that of the Logos. So, instead of being *anhypostatos,* it is *enhypostatos.* But this

---

[44] *Not* Byzantium. Cf. Mascall, *Theology and the Gospel of Christ,* p. 242 (note 109).

suggestion[45] has been criticised on several grounds. First, it is said to come very close to Apollinarianism, although McIntyre points out that 'while Leontius affirms that the Logos takes human nature, Apollinarius speaks more specifically of the *flesh*'; so Leontius' position 'only resembles that of Apollinarius in so far as both of them omit from Christ's person the human ego'. Secondly, W. N. Pittenger (who puts great emphasis on this last point) insists that Leontius still leaves Christ's human nature without any strictly personal centre on which his human experiences can 'home'.[46] Thirdly, McIntyre argues that on this basis the 'particularity and individuality of the man Jesus would be removed. In fact, it would be impossible to differentiate the *man* Jesus from the man Peter or the man John unless, in some way, the human *hypostasis* were retained.' Lastly, he insists, it puts our whole redemption in jeopardy on the principle that 'what Christ did not take, he did not redeem'. But it may be observed in passing that it does not seem to me that these arguments are by any means unanswerable.[47]

A different attempt to come to terms with this problem was made by Ephraim of Antioch, who maintained, in conformity with Chalcedonian orthodoxy, that the two natures were not to be divided, since 'two natures does not mean two *hypostases*'. But he then explains that 'while the two natures as such are not confused or compounded, the two *hypostases* are'. So the *hypostasis* of Christ 'is a fusion of the human and the divine *hypostasis*'. About this McIntyre remarks that, by thus insisting on the presence, in the composite *hypostasis,* of the human *hypostasis,* this theory 'secures the wholeness of the humanity which Jesus Christ took, and firmly avoids the docetic and Apollinarian tendencies of the enhypostatic theory. Jesus Christ is a real man, not simply *humanitas* or the *humanum*'. It also, on the strictly technical side, 'serves to protect Chalcedon from the

---

[45] Which would seem to be the only reasonable explanation of what Cyril must have meant by the phrase 'impersonal human nature'. Cf. pp. 145f. below.

[46] Cf. *The Word Incarnate* (Nisbet, 1959), pp. 100-3.

[47] See, in part, the last chapter in this book.

common charge that it operates with an 'impersonal' view of the human nature of Jesus Christ'.[48] But, however this may be, the major objection to this whole argument is that it is based on a philosophical approach and framework which is alien to us today.

The strength of the Nestorian position is that it does at least attempt to give full weight to the fact that, whatever else may be postulated of the Jesus of the Gospels, he was beyond question a man – as all his disciples would have recognised. The strength of the Monophysite view, on the other hand, is that he was also unmistakably one person, not two. The Chalcedonian Definition, by contrast, leaves him very much a philosophical abstraction,[49] admirably though it guards orthodoxy against a number of distortions and aberrations. Curiously enough, the Monophysites and Nestorians come comparatively close together when the former declare that the two natures 'can be distinguished only in theory', and when the latter insist that 'nature' and 'person' are almost equivalent in this context. But the fact remains that the Monophysites end up with a Christ who is not really a man, and the Nestorians with a figure who is not an integrated personality. Always, it would seem, there was an element of falsehood, as well as partial truth, on both sides of the controversy. This can be seen, yet again, in the dispute between the Monothelites and the Dyothelites in the seventh century as to whether Jesus had one will or two, human and divine; for the Monothelites could point to the testimony of the New Testament to Jesus' unswerving obedience to the Father as evidence of a *unity* of will, while the Dyothelites could argue that the voluntary *capacity* is 'inherent in an intelligent being as a function of its nature',[50] and that Jesus must have had a human will. As so often, the New Testament pinpoints the truth – and omits the error – of both sides when it records that Jesus prayed, in the

---

[48] Cf. *The Shape of Christology*, pp. 82-100.

[49] Expressed, moreover, in terms of a philosophical framework in which we do not normally think today.

[50] Cf. Pannenberg, *op. cit.*, p. 293.

garden of Gethsemane, 'that, if it were possible, this hour might pass him by. "Abba, Father", he said, "all things are possible to thee; take this cup away from me. Yet not what I will, but what thou wilt".'[51] Here we can certainly discern a human will, but one which was wholly subjected to that of the Father.

By and large, the Reformers accepted the classical Christology and made no attempt to change it. But it is significant that Luther put a particular emphasis on four points. First, he emphasised the humanity of Christ in his basic approach. 'The Scriptures', he observes,

> begin very gently, and lead us on to Christ as to a man, and then to one who is Lord over all creatures, and after that to one who is God. So do I enter delightfully, and learn to know God. But the philosophers and doctors have insisted on beginning from above; and so they have become fools. We must begin from below, and after that come upwards.

So he emphasised that Jesus 'ate, drank, slept and waked; was weary, sad, joyous; wept, laughed; was hungry, thirsty, cold; sweated, talked, worked, prayed'. Indeed, 'there was no difference between Him and other men save that He was God and without sin'. Secondly, he insisted that our redemption depends utterly on the deity of Christ, for sinners are guilty, and only God could save us. 'If Deity be wanting in Christ there is no help or deliverance for us against God's anger and judgments,' he wrote; so 'if it could not be held that God died for us, but only a man, then we are lost.' Thirdly, Luther insisted on the vital connection between Christ's person and his work: between the reality of the Incarnation and the efficacy of the Atonement – as will be apparent from what has already been quoted. Fourthly, his whole religion was supremely christocentric. 'I have no God, whether in heaven or earth, and I know of none,

---

[51] Mark 14:35f. NEB.

outside the flesh that lies in the bosom of the Virgin Mary. For elsewhere God is utterly incomprehensible, but comprehensible in the flesh of Christ alone,' he wrote; or, again, 'Wilt thou go surely and meet and grasp God rightly, so finding grace and help in him, be not persuaded to seek him elsewhere than in the Lord Christ. Let thine art and study begin with Christ, and there let it stay and cling.'

But in regard to the details of christological controversy, Luther adopted an essentially experiential and devotional, rather than abstract and philosophical, approach. He apparently accepted the dogma of the 'impersonality' of Christ's human nature, although this seems to have made little difference to him in practice.

> Christ is not called Christ because he has two natures. What is that to me? That he is by nature God and man is for himself. But what gives me comfort and blessing is that he so applies his office and pours forth his love and becomes my Saviour and Redeemer.

Yet Harnack could write of Luther that 'Since Cyril, no teacher has arisen in the Church to whom the mystery of the unity of the two natures in Christ was so deep a consolation'. For unity there certainly was, in Luther's view, since he reacted strongly against the Zwinglian teaching that it is only a figure of speech that we can assert an interchange of qualities between the two natures: 'If I believe that the human nature alone suffered for me,' Luther asserted, 'then is Christ worse than no Saviour to me.'[52]

But Lutheran doctrine, as it developed after Luther, became immersed in further dialectical refinements. One dispute was resolved by the Formula of Concord, in 1577; but a further controversy soon ensued, between the theologians of Tübingen and those of Giessen, about whether the incarnate Lord, in the days of his earthly life, actually renounced the use of his divine powers (which both

---

[52] Mackintosh, *op. cit.*, pp. 230-237.

sides agreed that he still possessed), or merely employed them secretly. The theologians of Giessen took the first view, and those of Tübingen the second; for the latter maintained that the child Jesus, *qua* man, in secret ruled the universe, and that he later, at times, exhibited omnipotence, omniscience and omnipresence. This controversy was ended by the *decisio Saxonica* in 1624, which basically accepted the view of Giessen (in Pannenberg's words)

> in rejecting a mere concealment *(krypsis)* of the possession and use of the divine attributes of majesty in Jesus' human nature during his earthly life and affirming a real renunciation *(kenosis)* of their use in the state of humiliation.[53]

But Mackintosh asserts that even the theologians of Giessen saw the 'humiliation' of the incarnate Saviour

> solely in this, that while retaining possession of the Divine qualities conveyed to His humanity by its union with the Logos, He yet made no habitual use of them. . .and only at times did His real powers flash through the veil.[54]

In the light of this, it is not altogether surprising that Lutheran theology was accused of being heir to the Monist traditions of Alexandria – and, indeed, of occasionally showing distinctly Monophysite tendencies. By contrast, 'Reformed' Christology might be said partially to have retained the traditions of Antioch; and it certainly held rigidly to the Chalcedonian Definition. It understood the *kenōsis*, or humiliation of Christ, in terms of the Incarnation itself; and it insisted that the Logos, although he had not divested himself of his essential deity (with all that this entails), had conjoined with himself a manhood that was

---

[53] Pannenberg, *op. cit.,* pp. 308f.
[54] Mackintosh, *op. cit.,* pp. 238-242.

truly human, of one substance with our own.[55] By contrast with the Lutherans, therefore, they were sometimes accused of having destroyed the unity of Christ's person, and even of Nestorian tendencies.

We must return to the Kenotic Theory in the last chapter of this book. Suffice it to say here that any theory which pictures one who was originally God, but who temporarily renounced his deity for the period of his earthly life, only to resume it at his ascension, is totally unacceptable. Even the Credal statement that the eternal Son 'came down from heaven' introduces what may be termed 'mythological' imagery which does not adequately convey the essential doctrine of the Incarnation: that *God himself, in the 'person' of the Son, actually became truly man without ceasing to be God.* I think Pannenberg is right, moreover, when he insists that many of our christological problems arise from an attempt to conceive some conjunction of the divine and the human in abstract terms, instead of starting with 'the concrete person of Jesus of Nazareth' and then finding ourselves forced to say, about him and him alone, that he is not only truly man but also truly God.[56] In terms of the classical Christology, what we must take from the Alexandrians is that Jesus Christ himself, and not merely the Logos who assumed manhood in him, was truly God; and what we must take from the Antiochenes is that he himself, as an integrated personality, truly *became* man. And we must also emphasise that there is an essential identity between the pre-existent Logos/Son and the incarnate Lord, both in his state of 'humiliation' and present 'exaltation'.

We must now turn, for the next three chapters, to see what has been made of this mystery by several participants in the contemporary debate – before attempting to discover whether some other solution is not more biblical, more viable and more adequate.

3
The Incarnation and Comparative Religion

IN MY LAST CHAPTER I TRIED TO SUMMARISE SOME OF THE
christological controversies which culminated in the Nicene
Creed and the Definition of Chalcedon, the continuing
disputes in the Churches of the East and West about how
these statements should be understood, and the renewed
debates and disagreements which followed the Reformation. Almost inevitably, I think, some of the extravagances,
contradictions and seeming quibbles of this age-long
attempt to plumb the mystery of the Incarnation leave us,
today, dissatisfied and disturbed. It is not only the hair-
splitting and *odium theologicum* of those often bitter wars
of words which distress us, but the seeming unreality of the
philosophical straight-jacket of the classical formulations.
Instinctively, we long to get back to the vitality, and
apparent simplicity, of the New Testament; to approach its
records and statements with an open mind; and to do our
utmost to come to at least a tentative understanding of this
mystery in a way that satisfies our minds and our hearts. So
in my next two chapters I shall discuss a few recent attempts
to do this; and then, in my final chapter, I shall venture to
outline the way in which I have myself come to approach this
whole subject.

But we live today in a pluralist society in which we are
aware, in a new way, of what other men believe. It is
essential, therefore, to try to view the New Testament
against the background of other religions. What light, if any,
do the 'Mystery religions', some of which preceded the
apostolic *kerygma*, and continued for a number of years to
vie with it for men's allegiance, throw on the Incarnation?
Has the history of Mahāyāna Buddhism, perhaps, anything

60

to teach us about the way in which christological thought developed in the Christian Church? What, too, of the *avatars* of the gods (or of the 'Ultimate Reality') which occupy so prominent a place in the Hindu classics; or of the austere monotheism of the Qur'ān? Books, monographs and lectures on such subjects follow each other in endless succession today, one of the more recent of which is the book of essays entitled – somewhat provocatively – *The Myth of God Incarnate*. So it is to this book – or rather to the chapter on 'Jesus and the World Religions' contributed by its editor, Professor John Hick of Birmingham – that I shall now turn.

Hick does not deal in this chapter with the Mystery religions, both Hellenistic and Oriental, which claimed so many adherents around the Mediterranean basin at the beginning of the Christian era – although one of the other contributors, Dr. Francis Young, does allude to them;[1] but of their superficial resemblance to the new faith there can be little question. Basically nature religions and vegetation rites in origin, they mostly centred round a 'saviour god' – with or without a mother, consort or other figure – who died and then came to life again; and in their more spiritual and sophisticated form they held out a promise not only of physical renewal and fertility but of future immortality. Two or three of them, moreover, even postulate an interval of about three days between the death and the revival of their saviour-god – a fact which has inevitably been linked with the New Testament witness to the resurrection of Christ on the third day. But Professor B. M. Metzger has emphasised that the evidence for the commemoration of the Hilaria, or the coming back to life of Attis, for example, cannot be traced back beyond the latter half of the second century A.D., and in the case of Adonis, too, such references as there are date from the second to the fourth century A.D.; whereas the categorical affirmation in 1 Corinthians 15 that Christ 'was raised to life on the third day' can be confidently

---

[1] They are mentioned briefly in one of Frances Young's contributions to *The Myth of God Incarnate*, pp. 102ff.

dated in the middle of the *first* century. If there was borrowing in this respect, therefore, it seems clear enough which way it went. Of Osiris, too, Metzger writes that 'after his consort Isis had sought and re-assembled thirteen of the fourteen pieces into which his body had been dismembered by his wicked brother. . . , through the help of magic she was enabled to re-animate his corpse'; and the contrast between this and the testimony of the apostolic Church to the resurrection of Jesus is obvious. In those Mystery religions which speak of a dying god, moreover, he 'died by compulsion and not by choice', and never in 'self-giving love'. But the fundamental difference between all the Mysteries and the Christian faith is that the former speak of a purely mythological figure who symbolises the death of nature in winter and its revival at the turn of the year, whereas the primitive Church testified to the resurrection 'on the third day' of a historical person whom they had both known and loved.[2]

Much the same can be said of the *avatars* of Hinduism. To begin with, they represent theophanies or 'descents' of the gods[3] in human guise – in a way to which the only parallel in Christianity would be the most extreme form of Docetism. They are, moreover, acknowledged by all educated Hindus to be purely mythological – that is, in Professor Hick's use of the word myth, 'a story which is told but which is not literally true'. Bishop Lesslie Newbigin, indeed, writes that he has never forgotten the astonishment with which a devout and learned teacher of the Rāmakrishna Mission regarded him when he discovered that Newbigin was prepared to rest his 'whole faith as a Christian upon the substantial historical truth of the record concerning Jesus in the New Testament'. To the Hindu it 'seemed axiomatic that such vital matters of religious truth could not be allowed to depend upon the accidents of history. If the truths which Jesus exemplified and taught are true, then they are true always and everywhere, whether a person called Jesus ever lived or not'.

[2] Cf. B. M. Metzger.
[3] Or, in the view of more sophisticated Hindus, of the 'Ultimate Reality'.

But there is all the difference in the world between a statement about the nature of God – or a purely mythical *avatar* to illustrate some aspect of that nature – and

> a report that God has, at a certain time and place, acted in a certain way. In the latter case the occurrence is the essence of the message. The care which is taken in the New Testament to place the events recorded in the continuum of secular history is in striking contrast to the indifference which is generally shown with regard to the historicity of the events which Hindu piety loves to remember in connection with the character of the gods. There is no serious attempt to relate them to events in secular history, nor is it felt that there would be any advantage to be gained from trying to do so – even if it could be done.

Their value is that they illustrate truths about God which would remain true whether or not these particular events had ever actually happened.[4]

But Professor Hick fails to make any distinction between the purely mythological nature of Hindu *avatars* and the basic historicity of the founder of Buddhism – to say nothing of Christianity. Instead, he insists that

> we should never forget that if the Christian gospel had moved east, into India, instead of west, into the Roman empire, Jesus' religious significance would probably have been expressed by hailing him within Hindu culture as a divine Avatar and within the Mahāyāna Buddhism which was then developing in India as a Bodhisattva, one who has attained to oneness with Ultimate Reality but remains in the human world out of compassion for mankind and to show others the way of life. These would have been the *appropriate* expressions, within these cultures, of the *same* spiritual reality.[5]

---

[4] Cf. *The Finality of Christ* (SCM Press, 1969), pp. 50ff.
[5] *Op. cit.*, p. 176. My italics.

Yet he unequivocally affirms that 'Jesus was a real man who really lived in first century Palestine',[6] and that 'we receive, mainly from the Synoptic Gospels, an impression of a real person with a real message'[7] – although he positively goes to town about 'how fragmentary and ambiguous are the data available to us as we try to look back across nineteen and a half centuries', and 'how large and variable is the contribution of the imagination to our "pictures" of Jesus.'[8] It is, of course, eminently salutary to be reminded how easy it is to construct a Jesus in one's own image, or at least according to one's own preconceived ideas; but I have certainly never heard him described as 'a stern lawgiver and implacable judge',[9] and Hick greatly exaggerates the paucity of positive evidence we have about the one to whom he refers as 'the largely unknown man of Nazareth'.[10]

He himself, he tells us, sees

> the Nazarene, then, as intensely and overwhelmingly conscious of the reality of God. He was a man of God, living in the unseen presence of God, and addressing God as *abba,* father... He was so powerfully God-conscious that his life vibrated, as it were, to the divine life; and as a result his hands could heal the sick, and the 'poor in spirit' were kindled to new life in his presence. If you or I had met him in first-century Palestine we would – we may hope – have felt deeply disturbed and challenged by his presence. We would have felt the absolute claim of God confronting us, summoning us to give ourselves wholly to him and to be born again as his children and as agents of his purposes on earth... And such is the intereaction of body and mind that in deciding to give ourselves to God, in response to his claim mediated through Jesus,

[6] *Ibid.,* p. 168.
[7] *Ibid.,* p. 172.
[8] *Ibid.,* p. 167.
[9] *Ibid.*
[10] *Ibid.,* p. 168. Contrast the remarks of A.N. Sherwin White in *Roman Society and Roman Law in the New Testament* (Oxford, Clarendon, 1963), pp. 187ff.

we might have found ourselves trembling or in tears, or uttering the strange sounds that are called speaking with tongues. . . .[11]

'If this interpretation is at all on the right lines,' he later affirms, 'Jesus cannot have failed to be aware that he was himself far more intensely conscious of God, and that he was far more faithfully obedient to God, than could be said of any contemporaries whom he had met or of whom he had heard.' Indeed,

> he was himself directly and overwhelmingly conscious of the heavenly Father, so he could speak about him with authority, could summon men and women to live as his children, could declare his judgment and his forgiveness, and could heal the sick by his power. Jesus must thus have been conscious of a unique position among his contemporaries, which he may have expressed by accepting the title of Messiah or, alternatively, by applying to himself the image of the heavenly Son of Man – two categories each connoting a human being called to be God's special servant and agent on earth.[12]

So much for the historic Jesus, as Hick sees him. But then, he believes, the Church embarked on a gradual process of deifying him, in a way to which he sees a reasonably close parallel, *mutatis mutandis,* in the deification of Gautama – who, too, 'was a real historical individual who lived in north-east India from about 563 to about 483 B.C.', but who made no claim to be divine.[13] In the 'earliest Christian preaching, as we have echoes of it in Acts', he writes, 'Jesus was proclaimed as "a man attested to you by God with mighty works and wonders and signs" (Acts 2:22)', whereas 'some thirty years later the Gospel of Mark could

---

[11] *Ibid.,* p. 172.
[12] *Ibid.,* p. 173.
[13] *Ibid.,* pp. 168ff.

open with the words "The beginning of the gospel of Jesus Christ, the Son of God. . ." And in John's Gospel, written after another thirty or so years' development, this Christian language is attributed to Jesus himself and he is depicted as walking the earth as a consciously divine being'.[14] This dramatic change, he suggests, must be explained in terms of Jesus' 'tremendous spiritual power';[15] of 'some kind of experience of seeing Jesus after his death, an appearance or appearances which came to be known as his resurrection'[16] (to which we must soon revert); and of pressures that must soon have developed 'to use titles which would more explicitly present the challenge of Jesus' saving power' – and 'these could only be the highest titles available'.[17] Ideas of divinity embodied in human life were widespread in the ancient world, we are told, so 'there is nothing in the least surprising in the deification of Jesus in that cultural environment'.[18] Within Judaism the King was at times designated, metaphorically, as the 'son' of Yahweh – to say nothing of pagan practice in the Roman empire – so it was natural enough, the argument runs, for this title to be applied to Jesus, once the Church came to regard him as the Messiah; but Hick thinks it probable that it was 'only with the stories of the Virgin Birth of Jesus in Matthew's and Luke's Gospels that the Lord's anointed is thought of within Israel as physically *(sic!)* God's son'.[19] Then, as Christian theology 'grew through the centuries, it made the very significant transition from "Son of God" to "God the Son", the Second Person of the Trinity' – although Hick concedes that the 'transposition of the poetic image, son of God, into the trinitarian concept, God the Son, is already present in the fourth Gospel'.[20] It was in some such way as this, he believes,

[14] *Ibid.*, p. 173.
[15] *Ibid.*
[16] *Ibid.*, p. 170.
[17] *Ibid.*, p. 174.
[18] *Ibid.* See also Frances Young's account of philosophers, Emperors and 'divine men' to whom a miraculous birth, or some sort of 'divinity', was attributed (*Ibid.*, pp. 93ff.).
[19] *Ibid.*, p. 175.
[20] *Ibid.*

that we can explain how the Church came '*ultimately* to the point of deification'.[21]

But the trouble with this superficially plausible reconstruction is that the evidence, as I see it, does not support it – and actually points in the opposite direction – in point after point.[22] Even in the very sermon recorded in Acts 2 from which Hick quotes what he terms 'echoes of the earliest Christian preaching', for example, Peter refers to Jesus as having been 'raised up' and 'exalted at the right hand of God', and declares 'Let all the house of Israel therefore know assuredly that God has made him both Lord and Christ, this Jesus whom you crucified'.[23] A little later in the same book, moreover, we read that Peter affirms that 'there is salvation in no one else, for there is no other name under heaven given among men by which we must be saved' – and we find that the early disciples found it perfectly natural to address prayer to the 'Lord Jesus'.[24] But it is astonishing how some scholars give enormous emphasis to statements in Acts which suit their own thesis, and completely ignore those that do not.

It seems to me, moreover, that this reconstruction flies in the face of the evidence when the stories of the Virgin Birth are regarded as giving rise to a significant change of attitude. While I myself fully accept these stories as historical, it seems obvious that it is on the person of Jesus, and on his death and resurrection, that the whole emphasis in the apostolic *kerygma* was placed; and it is, perhaps, relevant in this context that no direct reference to the Virgin Birth is made in John's Gospel, to which Hick attributes so fundamental a role in depicting Jesus, in phraseology which surely represents something of a caricature, as 'walking the earth as a consciously divine being'.[25]

But Hick deals with the available evidence in a still more

---

[21] *Ibid.*, p. 173. My italics.
[22] This point has been very recently emphasised in an article in *The Times Higher Education Supplement* (23 Dec 1977) by Professor C. F. D. Moule.
[23] Acts 2:31-36.
[24] Acts 4:12 and 7:59.
[25] *Op. cit.*, p. 173. For a discussion of this point see pp. 147ff, etc., below.

cavalier fashion. He gives much prominence to the Fourth Gospel in paving the way for what he terms the ultimate deification of Jesus, and he dates this Gospel – with most, but by no means all, contemporary scholars – in the last decade of the first century; but he continually ignores both the evidence of the Pauline epistles some forty years earlier and also that of the letter to the Hebrews – which *must*, I should have thought, be dated before the fall of Jerusalem in 70 A.D. In 1 Thessalonians, which is commonly regarded as the earliest of Paul's letters, for example, we read that the Thessalonians had come to serve 'the living and true God, and to wait expectantly for the appearance from heaven of his Son Jesus, whom he raised from the dead, Jesus our deliverer from the terrors of judgment to come'.[26] For those who regard the Epistle to the Galatians as even earlier, moreover, reference can be made to a number of similar verses – notably, perhaps, the statement that 'God sent his own Son, born of a woman, born under the law, to purchase freedom for the subjects of the law, in order that we might attain the status of sons'.[27] In the Epistle to the Colossians, again, we read (in reference to God's 'dear Son') that 'He is the image of the invisible God; his is the primacy over all created things. In him everything in heaven and on earth was created. . . And he exists before everything, and all things are held together in him'.[28] The Epistle to the Hebrews, too, speaks in much the same way when it declares that 'When in former times God spoke to our forefathers, he spoke in fragmentary and varied fashion through the prophets. But in this the final age he has spoken to us in the Son whom he has made heir to the whole universe, and through whom he created all orders of existence: the Son who is the effulgence of God's splendour and the stamp of God's very being, and sustains the universe by his word of power'.[29] To put such an emphasis on John's Gospel, therefore, and completely to

---

[26] 1 Thess 1:9f. NEB.
[27] Gal. 4:4 and 5 NEB.
[28] Col. 1:15-17 NEB.
[29] Hebrews 1:1-3.

ignore the earlier, and almost equally explicit, contribution of Paul and Hebrews to the 'ultimate' deification of Jesus, seems to me to represent a singularly arbitrary selection of evidence – to say nothing of verses in the Synoptic Gospels such as 'Everything is entrusted to me by my Father; and no one knows who the Son is but the Father, or who the Father is but the Son, and those to whom the Son may choose to reveal him'.[30] When, moreover, Hick suggests a parallel between the development of christological thought in the Christian Church and that of the Mahāyāna Buddhist concept of the 'heavenly Buddha', he fails to point out that, whereas the Christian view goes right back to the first generation of Christians, the fact that the Buddhist concept 'began to develop at about the same time as Christianity'[31] – as he puts it – means that this happened some five centuries after Gautama's death.

Hick also asserts that 'There can I think be no doubt that this deification of Jesus came about partly – and perhaps mainly – as a result of the Christian experience of reconciliation with God'. He rightly emphasises the disciples' 'glorious sense of the divine forgiveness and love' and the fact that the 'early Christian community lived and rejoiced in the knowledge of God's accepting grace'. There was thus, he argues, 'a natural transition in their minds from the experience of reconciliation with God as Jesus' disciples, to the thought of his death as an atoning sacrifice, and from this to the conclusion that in order for Jesus' death to have been a sufficient atonement for human sin he must himself have been divine'.[32]

Now this, as I see it, is an exceedingly important point to which I shall return later, for it is significant that in books and discussions about comparative religion the major emphasis is almost always put on the need for a divine self-revelation, rather than on the equally basic need for an atonement for sin. But when Hick argues that the influence

[30] Luke 10:22. Cf. Matt. 11:27 NEB.
[31] *Op. cit.*, pp. 168f.
[32] *Op. cit.*, p. 170.

of 'a long tradition of priestly sacrifice', and the thought that 'without the shedding of blood there is no forgiveness of sins',[33] led naturally to 'this deification of Jesus', he omits to note that the Synoptic Gospels record that Jesus himself said that 'the Son of Man did not come to be served but to serve, and to surrender his life as a ransom for many'[34] and also, at the Last Supper, that 'this is my blood, the blood of the covenant, shed for many for the forgiveness of sins'.[35] The first of these recorded statements is almost certainly an echo of Isaiah 53, which (as Dr. Vincent Taylor has persuasively argued) seems to have dominated Jesus' understanding of his messianic mission and also its interpretation by the early Church[36] – and which was, it would seem, something which the risen Lord specifically explained to his disciples.[37]

But this brings us inevitably to the resurrection, which was almost certainly the basic reason why the disciples began to confess that 'Jesus is Lord', to apply to him references to Yahweh in the Old Testament, and to have no hesitation in worshipping him and addressing him in prayer. Hick rightly remarks that it will be said that 'there is at least one all-important difference between Jesus and Gautama which justifies the ascription of divine attributes to the one and not to the other – namely that Jesus rose from the dead. Does not his resurrection set him apart from all other men and show him to be God incarnate? Such an argument inevitably suggests itself'. But he immediately adds that this argument 'proves difficult to sustain'[38] – to which the obvious reply is that he himself certainly makes exceedingly heavy weather of the way in which he deals both with what he terms 'the resurrection event', and with its nature and implications.

First, he asserts that the 'possibilities range from the resuscitation of Jesus' corpse to visions of the Lord in

---

[33] *Op. cit.,* p. 176.
[34] Mark 10:45 NEB.
[35] Matt. 26:28 NEB.
[36] Cf. Luke 22:37; 1 Peter 2:24f; etc.
[37] Cf. Luke 24:44ff.
[38] *Op. cit.,* p. 170.

resplendent glory'.[39] But it seems perfectly clear that the records do not point to a resuscitated corpse, and that they go distinctly beyond mere visions. In regard to the first suggestion, there can, I think, be little doubt that St. Paul was thinking of the risen Redeemer as well as the future state of the redeemed when he made a clear-cut distinction between a 'natural' or 'animal' body and a 'spiritual' body[40]; and this seems to be confirmed by his teaching that 'Christ, once raised from the dead, is never to die again: he is no longer under the dominion of death',[41] and that 'the Lord Jesus Christ. . . will transfigure the body belonging to our humble state, and give it a form like that of his own resplendent body'.[42] It is in this context that Wolfhart Pannenberg writes:

> The notion of the resurrection of the dead that is most obvious on the basis of the analogy of sleeping and waking would be that of a revivification of the corpse in the sense of what has died standing up and walking around. It is, however, absolutely certain that the resurrection of the dead was not understood in this way in the primitive Christian and, in any case, in the oldest, the Pauline, concept. For Paul, resurrection means the new life of a new body, not the return of life into a dead but not yet decayed fleshly body. . . It is self-evident for him that the future body will be a different one from the present body, . . .not perishable but imperishable in glory and power, not a fleshly body equipped with a soul but a spiritual body.[43]

Then he adds:

> The explications in 1 Cor. 15:35-56 are not especially concerned with the resurrection of Jesus Christ, but

[39] *Ibid.*
[40] 1 Cor. 15:44-55.
[41] Rom. 6:9 NEB.
[42] Phil. 3:21 NEB.
[43] *Jesus – God and Man* (SCM Press, London, 1968), p. 75.

with the resurrection that Christians expect in the future. But Paul must have had the same conception of the resurrected Jesus, for he always and fully thought about Jesus' resurrection and that of Christians in essential parallel. It is particularly significant that Paul understood the resurrection of the dead, and so also the resurrection of Jesus, not as mere resuscitation of a corpse but as a radical transformation.[44]

And the way in which the resurrection appearances recorded in the Gospels depict the risen Lord as passing through closed doors – or now appearing and now disappearing – certainly supports this view.

The primary argument against the 'resurrection-event' being understood merely in terms of 'visions of the Lord in resplendent glory', on the other hand, is the evidence that the tomb was in fact empty – and the evidence for this is exceedingly strong. First, there is the positive evidence. Mark's Gospel, in its original form, probably ends with the women's visit to the tomb from which the body had disappeared. Matthew and Luke add rather more details – about which I will content myself, in this context, with stating that I am convinced that the alleged contradictions between the different accounts have been much exaggerated, and that some of the glosses put on the additional material in Matthew are very far fetched – e.g. Christopher Evans' remark that 'The guards at the sealed tomb, who are found only in Matthew's version, together with the women, who because of the sealing of the tomb can now come only to visit it and not to anoint the body, become spectators of a divine miracle'. On this particular flight of scholarly fancy I will repeat the comment that I made some years ago:

> But Matthew tells us that the Chief Priests asked Pilate to set a guard over the tomb on the day *after* the burial, so the women could scarcely have known about this;

[44] *Op. cit.*, p. 76.

and there is no conclusive reason why they should not have come to add their 'spices and ointments' (as recorded in Luke 23:56) to those hastily provided by Nicodemus (as recorded in John 19:39) on the Friday evening. Nor is it at all necessary to assume, from this very concise account, that the women had already arrived at the tomb when the earthquake is said to have occurred and the angel to have rolled away the stone. It is intrinsically unlikely, on any showing, that the angel would address the women, in the manner recorded, in the presence of the guards – and there are a number of ways in which the story of the earthquake, and how the angel rolled away the stone, might have become known. It is perfectly possible, moreover, to regard Matthew 28:2-4 as a sort of parenthesis.[45]

And in John's Gospel we have the vivid account of how Mary Magdalene was the first to arrive at the tomb, saw that the stone had been rolled away, and ran to call Peter and 'the disciple whom Jesus loved'; how they set out to the tomb, and in their eagerness began to run; how 'the other disciple', younger than Peter, got there first, stooped down and peered into the tomb, but characteristically did not go in; how Peter, equally characteristically, blundered straight in, followed by his companion; how they both took note of 'the linen cloths lying, and the napkin, which had been on [Jesus'] head, not lying with the linen cloths but rolled up in a place by itself'; and how John (presumably), when he saw this, at once 'believed' in the resurrection. On this story William Temple comments: 'It is most manifestly the record of a personal memory. Nothing else can account for the little details, so vivid, so little like the kind of thing that comes from invention or imagination.'[46]

[45] Cf. *A Lawyer among the Theologians* (Hodder and Stoughton, London, 1973), pp. 144f. – together with footnotes. In this book I have attempted to discuss this whole matter in much greater detail than is feasible here.
[46] Cf. John 20:1-10, and William Temple, *Readings in St. John's Gospel* (Macmillan, London, 1949), p. 376.

Then why, it has often been asked, is there no mention of the empty tomb in the earliest tradition about the resurrection to come down to us   in 1 Corinthians 15:3-8? To this the obvious answer is that, while there is no explicit statement that the tomb was empty, there is a most convincing implicit reference to this fact; for what Oriental Jew of the first century could possibly have written that 'Christ died for our sins' (physically, of course), that 'he was buried' (again, physically, of course), and that he was then 'raised to life on the third day', if he had not believed that *something* had happened to the body? This would be a most unnatural way of recording a tradition about a purely 'spiritual' survival of Jesus. Surely we must assume that it was the crucified and buried body which was both transformed and 'raised'? There would, moreover, have been no point whatever in saying that this happened 'on the third day' if the reference had been to mere spiritual survival.

This positive evidence is buttressed, moreover, by a considerable amount of what may be termed negative or circumstantial evidence. First, as Paul Althaus puts it: 'In Jerusalem, the place of Jesus' execution and grave, it was proclaimed not long after his death that he had been raised. The situation *demands* that within the circle of the first community one had a reliable testimony for the fact that the grave had been found empty.' This resurrection kerygma, he says, 'could not have been maintained in Jerusalem for a single day, for a single hour, if the emptiness of the tomb had not been established as a fact for all concerned'.[47] Again, Pannenberg insists that:

> Among the general historical arguments that speak for the trustworthiness of the report about the discovery of Jesus' tomb is, above all, the fact that the early Jewish polemic against the Christian message about Jesus' resurrection, traces of which have already been left in the Gospels, does not offer any suggestion that Jesus'

[47] *Die wahrheit des Kirchlichen Osterglambeus*, pp. 22ff. – as quoted by Pannenberg, *op. cit.*, p. 100.

grave had remained untouched. The Jewish polemic would have had to have every interest in the preservation of such a report. However, quite to the contrary, it shared the conviction with its Christian opponents that Jesus' grave was empty. It limited itself to explaining this fact in its own way. . . .[48]

But this explanation of why the tomb was empty – namely, that the disciples came by night and stole the body – is totally unacceptable on both ethical and psychological grounds. And subsequent attempts to explain the emptiness of the tomb on a rationalistic basis – e.g. that of Kirsopp Lake, B.H. Streeter, Venturini, etc. – seem to me equally unconvincing.[49]

The evidence of the empty tomb, however, should never be taken in isolation, but in close connection with the records of the 'appearances' of the risen Lord. For these testify to two quite different facts: the appearances, that it was no resuscitated corpse which appeared to the disciples; the empty tomb, that it was no wholly incorporeal phantom, ghost or vision. The records state that the risen Christ could be clearly seen, recognised with some difficulty (for it must not be supposed that his transformed body was exactly like the body which had been buried), could invite a finger to explore the print of the nails, and could even eat a piece of fish – not, of course, because a 'spiritual body' had any need of physical food, but presumably in order that his bewildered disciples might have concrete evidence, when his visible presence was withdrawn, that their experience had been no mere vision, but an objective reality.

But Hick also places great emphasis on the fact that 'it must be doubted whether the resurrection event – whatever its nature – was seen by Jesus' contemporaries as guaranteeing his divinity'.[50] In support of this statement he refers to the account of the raising of Lazarus, of the widow's son at

[48] *Op. cit.,* p. 101.
[49] Cf. *A Lawyer among the Theologians,* pp. 120ff.
[50] *Op. cit.,* p. 170.

Nain, of Jairus' daughter, etc., and to somewhat similar stories in the Old Testament and even the sub-apostolic age; but he significantly fails to make any distinction whatever between such resuscitations to ordinary human life (followed no doubt by another, and final, experience of physical death) – and the resurrection of Jesus, in a spiritual body, to live 'in the power of an endless life'. It is certainly true, as Hick (quoting George Caird) insists, that no resuscitation of a friend or acquaintance would make us conclude that 'this acquaintance was divine'.[51] This could also be said even about a genuine resurrection, to which all Christians look forward one day; for such a resurrection proves the power and love of God, rather than the divinity of those concerned. But I would strongly challenge the assertion that Christ's resurrection was *not* 'seen by Jesus' contemporaries as guaranteeing his divinity', for St. Paul specifically states that the one who 'on the human level...was born of David's stock' was, 'on the level of the spirit – the Holy Spirit – declared Son of God by a mighty act in that he rose from the dead';[52] and there is ample supporting evidence for the fact that it was the resurrection which prompted them to call him 'Lord' and to feel free – and, indeed, compelled – to worship him. It is perfectly true, of course, that 'Jesus is not said to have risen in virtue of a divine nature which he himself possessed but to have been raised by God'.[53] Precisely; and we are told that the fact that God did so raise him manifested the fact that he was his Son. Jesus had, indeed, previously testified to having a unique relationship with his heavenly Father; he had claimed to forgive sins, which all Jews regarded as a divine prerogative; and he had spoken and acted with sublime authority – as is demonstrated by the hostility of the scribes and Pharisees and, supremely, by his crucifixion. If these claims had been false, he would in fact have been guilty of the 'blasphemy' with which he was charged. But would God have raised a blasphemer from the dead? Surely the fact

[51] *Ibid.,* p. 171.
[52] Rom. 1:3 NEB.
[53] *Op. cit.,* p. 171.

that God did so raise him – and it seems that Jesus had virtually staked his credibility on the assertion that he would, little though his disciples understood this – could be regarded as a divine authentication of who he was and of the validity of his claims. This, I am convinced, was how the apostolic Church saw it. To quote Pannenberg once more:

> Jesus' claim to authority, through which he put himself in God's place, was, as we saw in the discussion of the antitheses in the Sermon on the Mount, blasphemous for Jewish ears. Because of this, Jesus was then also slandered by the Jews before the Roman governor as a rebel. If Jesus really has been raised, this claim has been visibly and unambiguously confirmed by the God of Israel, who was allegedly blasphemed by Jesus. . . That the primitive Christian proclamation in fact understood Jesus' resurrection from the dead as the confirmation of his pre-Easter claim emerges above all in the speeches in Acts.[54]

They also clearly regarded the fact that God had raised him from the dead as authenticating the meaning and significance of his death. This was not that of another martyr, to be interpreted in terms of being 'faithful unto death' and setting a magnificent example. Instead it was, as he himself had said, a 'ransom for many', so that Paul could (and did) base his doctrine of justification by faith on the fact that the raising of Jesus to life proved that he had not 'died for our sins' in vain.

I have lingered somewhat on the subject of the resurrection because it is so decisive, in my view, not only in the context of 'Jesus and the World Religions' but in regard to the doctrine of the Incarnation as a whole. This is attested, in part, by the space given to the resurrection in Professor Geoffrey Lampe's latest book, *God as Spirit*,[55] and by the

[54] *Op. cit.*, pp. 67f. Pannenberg cites 'Acts 2:3; 3:15; 5:30f. *et al.*' But he also refers to 'the old expression that Jesus was shown to be justified in the Spirit' (1 Tim. 3:16 *(b)*).
[55] Clarendon Press, Oxford, 1977. Cf. pp. 145-161.

dramatic way in which his own views have changed since his dialogue with Professor Donald MacKinnon on this subject was published in 1966.[56] I hope to discuss this in a subsequent chapter, so must not be diverted at this point.

When, therefore, Professor Hick asks: 'Why and how did this deification take place?',[57] the answer – as I see it – is that the decisive point in the experience of the disciples, and in the way in which they regarded Jesus, was the resurrection; but that this should not be regarded as the time when they 'deified' him, but rather when God showed them, and they realised, who he really was and always had been. But this does not mean that, even after the resurrection, they looked back on Jesus in the days of his flesh as not having been genuinely human. Instead it means that they could (and did) believe that, though truly man, he was more than a 'mere' man; that he had come from God in a unique sense; and that now they felt compelled, in a way that they found difficult to explain, to identify him with God. There was nothing in the least 'not literally true'[58] about this conviction, or about the faith of the primitive Church that it was through his death alone that they had been 'reconciled to God' and had come to enjoy pardon and peace.

When Hick turns specifically again, towards the end of his paper, to other religions, his conclusions are in part wholly predictable and in part, as I see it, strangely naïve. Once he had dismissed the consistent New Testament witness to the uniqueness of the person of Christ as purely 'mythological', and the New Testament understanding of the significance of his death as a mistaken deduction from the Jewish sacrificial system, it was entirely predictable that he would take the view that the life of Jesus was merely 'one point at which the Logos – that is, God-in-relation-to-man – has acted',[59] and should put it on much the same level as 'other particular revelations of the Logos at work in human life – in the

---

[56] *The Resurrection* (Mowbray's London, 1966).
[57] *The Myth of God Incarnate*, p. 173.
[58] *Ibid.*, p. 178.
[59] *Ibid.*, p. 181.

Hebrew prophets, in the Buddha, in the *Upanishads* and the *Bhagavad Gita,* in the *Koran,* and so on';[60] and it was almost equally predictable that he would be satisfied with defining 'all salvation' as 'the creating of human animals into children of God'.[61] But he is naïve (and perhaps a little disingenuous?) when he suggests that the only alternative (for those who regard Christ alone as 'the effulgence of God's splendour and the stamp of God's very being', and his atoning death as the unique basis for reconciliation between a holy God and sinful men and women) is 'the negative assertion that the Logos has not acted and is not acting anywhere else in human life';[62] that 'the whole religious life of mankind, beyond the stream of Judaic-Christian faith, is thus by implication excluded as lying outside the sphere of salvation';[63] that 'the only doorway to eternal life is Christian faith';[64] and that God 'has decreed that only those born within one particular thread of human life should be saved'[65] – or, indeed, that the only escape from such a 'negative assertion' is the postulate that 'devout men of other faiths may be Christians without knowing it, or may be anonymous Christians. . .or may have implicit faith and receive baptism by desire, and so on'.[66] Surely he does not really think that to regard Christ as the unique revelation of God implies that God has wholly 'left himself without witness' in all non-Christian religions; or that to say that 'there is none other name[67] under heaven given among men by which we must be saved' means that all those who have not consciously put their faith in that name are necessarily 'lost'? What about all those Jews in Old Testament days who, convicted of sin, turned to God in repentance and

[60] *Ibid.*
[61] *Ibid.*
[62] *Ibid.*
[63] *Ibid.,* p. 179.
[64] *Ibid.,* p. 180.
[65] *Ibid.*
[66] *Ibid.*
[67] The 'name' to which reference is made in this statement is, of course, that of Jesus. But 'name' in the Bible stands for the person concerned: that is, who and what he is.

faith, and in suitable cases brought the prescribed sacrifices? Surely they were 'saved' – in spite of the fact that they had not been in a position to put their trust in the Christ who had not yet been born? Yet surely it was *through* him that they were accepted and forgiven, for the New Testament specifically tells us that 'he is the mediator of a new covenant' under which his atoning death brings 'deliverance from sins committed under the former covenant'.[68] So who would dare to say that the same principle may not be applicable to individuals from any culture or religion who, convicted of their sin and need by the Holy Spirit, turn to God – as best they know – in repentance and faith? To deny that there is any 'saving structure' in other religions as such, or to affirm that there is salvation in Christ alone, is not of itself to exclude any repentant sinner – or, indeed, babies, young children, imbeciles, etc. – from the scope of that salvation; and I emphatically deny that to believe this is an attempt 'to square an inadequate theology with the facts of God's world' or 'an anachronistic clinging to the husk of the old doctrine after its substance has crumbled.'[69]

We all admire tolerance and broad-mindedness, and we are justly suspicious of anything which savours of arrogance or dogmatism. But 'a Christianity which should think of itself as one of many diverse contributions to the religious life of mankind', Visser't Hooft insists, 'is a Christianity that has lost its foundation in the New Testament'.[70] It is inevitable, as Stephen Neill puts it, that the Christian faith

> casts the shadow of falsehood, or at least of imperfect truth, on every other system. This Christian claim is naturally offensive to the adherents of every other religious system. It is almost as offensive to modern man, brought up in the atmosphere of relativism, in which tolerance is regarded almost as the highest of the virtues. But we must not suppose that this claim to

[68] Heb. 9:15 NEB.
[69] *Op. cit.*, p. 180. I have discussed this question in some detail in the last chapter of *Christianity and Comparative Religion* (Tyndale Press, London, 1970).
[70] *No Other Name* (SCM Press, London, 1963), p. 117.

universal validity is something that can quietly be removed from the Gospel without changing it into something entirely different from what it is. The mission of Jesus was limited to the Jews and did not look immediately beyond them; but his life, his method and his message do not make sense, unless they are interpreted in the light of his own conviction that he was in fact the final and decisive word of God to men. . . For the human sickness there is one specific remedy, and this is it. There is no other.[71]

We can, however, wholeheartedly agree with Hick when he insists that 'from now onwards the Christian mission in lands dominated by any of the other world religions must rest upon the positive attraction of the person and teaching of Jesus and of the life lived in discipleship to him, and not upon the power of an alien culture seeking to impose itself upon politically vulnerable or economically less developed peoples'. It should, indeed, always have been so – and often, although by no means always, it was. As he justly says: 'The Jesus who is for the world is not the property of the human organisation called the Christian Church, nor is he to be confined within its theoretical constructions.'[72] But this does not in any way invalidate Lesslie Newbigin's assertion that 'acceptance of Jesus Christ as Lord means radical repentance and conversion from all pre-Christian religious experience' – even though the convert will often look back and trace the hand of God in these experiences. 'The focus of the Gospel', he continues, 'is the word of the cross, and that word is a radical judgment upon all human wisdom, and upon the experience on which that wisdom is founded. . . It is in the presence of the cross that we are compelled to say: "There is none righteous, no not one".[73]

[71] *Christian Faith and Other Faiths* (OUP, London, 1961), pp. 16f.
[72] *Op. cit.,* pp. 182f.
[73] *The Finality of Christ* (SCM Press, London, 1960), pp. 57f.

4
Some Examples of the Contemporary Debate I

IN MY LAST CHAPTER WE CONSIDERED THE INCARNATION in the context of other religions and, in particular, of the chapter on 'Jesus and World Religions' contributed by Professor John Hick to the symposium *The Myth of God Incarnate*. In this chapter and the next, however, we shall not be concerned with comparative religion, but Christology as such – and with the growing tendency, in more radical circles, for theologians to regard Jesus as a man, in himself exclusively human, in and through whom God acted in a special, or even unique, way. And I think that the fairest, and perhaps most useful, approach will be to examine in some detail the views of a very few representative theologians, as expressed chiefly in one or other of their comparatively recent books, rather than make an arbitrary selection of excerpts from a number of different writers. So in this present chapter we shall concentrate on two authors, Professor John Knox and Dr. John Robinson – both of them considerably more 'orthodox', I would think, than the majority of contributors to *The Myth of God Incarnate* – as they have expressed their views in *The Humanity and Divinity of Christ* and *The Human Face of God*, respectively.

Knox certainly goes much further than Hick when he states unequivocally that

> There is a divine and a human ingredient in the concrete reality of Christ. The Church's memory of Jesus is the memory of a man, a *human* being; its knowledge of the risen, living Lord is the knowledge of a *divine* being – still human, in a sense, since he is still the same being, but now *divinely* human. . . It is simply

82

a fact about us as Christians that we both look *back* to Jesus and look *up* to him. . . But the one we know in memory is fully human; the one we know in worship is *this same one* divinely exalted.[1]

He insists, moreover, that 'the acknowledging of this humanity and divinity of Christ, both in a full, unqualified sense, involves no necessary logical contradiction'. Instead, it represents, as it were, a partial return to what he sees as the 'adoptionist Christology' of the primitive Church; for

> The one it remembered as a man *had been* a man; the same one was now known as Lord and Christ because he *had in fact been made* Lord and Christ. This was, to be sure, a marvellous, and almost, incredible fact – nothing less than the miracle of the resurrection – but no logical difficulty was involved.[2]

About the 'miracle of the resurrection', moreover, Knox categorically asserts that

> one cannot escape the claim of the Gospel that this incident actually took place. No process of demythologisation which does away with the actuality of this occurrence can be true to the Gospel's intention. . . For how could Jesus, who was crucified, the remembered One, have become Christ, the living Lord, except through the interposition of some objective occurrence?

No one, of course, claimed to have actually seen the resurrection take place, but the disciples 'saw the risen Jesus (and there can be no doubt that they did!)'; so the fact of the resurrection is, he says, 'an inescapable implication of the Church's existence'.[3]

[1] *The Humanity and Divinity of Christ* (C.U.P., 1967), pp. 54f.
[2] *Op. cit.*, p. 55.
[3] *Ibid.*, p. 78.

But his attitude towards the pre-existence of the risen Lord, as we saw in my first chapter, is the precise opposite: for first he asserts that this 'cannot, in the nature of the case, be thus *known*'; then he questions 'whether the affirmation of it is essentially, or in principle, necessary';[4] and finally he insists that his pre-existence, in any sense other than the plan and purpose of God, cannot possibly be reconciled with his humanity – since 'there is no way of distinguishing Jesus' humanity from ours which does not deny that reality of his manhood in every sense which makes the affirmation of it significant'.[5]

When one begins to surmise why there is 'no logical difficulty' in a mere man, however wonderful, being raised to 'divinity' and Lordship, but an inherent *impossibility,* 'by definition', in God becoming man,[6] the answer Knox gives – in part, again – is that we should not ask 'Who *was* Christ?' but 'What was *happening* in Christ'.[7] In other words, the truth, he believes, is not that Jesus *was* 'very God of very God', but that

> the reality of God himself, 'very God of very God, ... came down from heaven' and was manifested, in mighty power, in an event which happened in and through and around this man and was embodied in a community which came to exist, and still exists, in and through and around this same man, raised from death and exalted.

So 'what more could have been said? What higher status could we have given him?'[8] But to this the answer seems obvious. It is abundantly clear that Knox, for all his insistence that the Church knows 'the risen, living Lord' as 'a *divine* being', or a '*divinely* human' being, does not believe that, even after his resurrection and exaltation, he has

4 *Ibid.,* p. 56.
5 *Ibid.,* p. 106.
6 Cf. pp. 55 and 67.
7 Cf. *ibid.,* p. 57.
8 *Ibid.,* p. 59.

'become God'; for he explicitly states that 'if it is impossible
to conceive that God could become a man, it is also
impossible to conceive of a man's becoming God'. Much
more impossible, most people would unhesitatingly affirm;
but to this point I must return later. In Knox's view,
however, 'no such conception needs to be involved in our
confession of the resurrection, as a result of which Jesus did
not become God but was 'raised to the *right hand* of God'.[9]
To whom, then, does the Church accord worship, and
address her prayers, when she prays, as she has always felt
free to pray, to the risen Lord? Is it to this 'divinely human'
being at God's right hand who is in no real sense identified
with God? Would not that be a form of idolatry? So is it,
perhaps, not to him, but merely to what 'happened' in him?
But can one really worship, or pray to, an event? Or is it in
fact to the God who acted in him, and to no one or nothing
else? If this is the real answer, then should we not recognise
that the instinct, and even the sense of compulsion, to
worship the 'Lord Jesus' is – and always has been – a dis-
astrous mistake? It is not enough for Knox to complain that
what happened is that the 'centre of interest' shifted, at an
early date, 'from the divine meaning of an event to the divine
nature of a person', and that the Church began to ask
whether the event was 'significant because of what God did
or because of what Jesus was';[10] for the answer to this is
surely that the significance of the event – the double 'event'
of God's self-revelation and work of redemption – is vitally
linked with the person through whom, and in whom, it was
effected.

The fact is that Knox, like many other theologians who
share his basic reasoning, is so obsessed by the conviction
that a Jesus who was truly man *could* not, of necessity, have
also been God in any essential, or ontological, sense, that he
lets this colour his whole approach to the New Testament.
He recognises, of course, that the records include a great
deal of material which is clearly inconsistent with his thesis;

[9] *Ibid.*, p. 111.
[10] *Ibid.*, p. 60.

but he is highly selective in the emphasis and significance he gives to one part of the evidence, and in the way in which he glosses, or sometimes ignores, the rest. And he does this, as far as I can see, purely on the subjective basis of his own theological or philosophical convictions, rather than any objective assessment – however critical – of the nature of the records or the weight of the evidence.[11] In the letter to the Hebrews, for example, he puts a paramount emphasis on those verses which state that 'a consecrating priest and those whom he consecrates are all of one stock';[12] so Jesus 'had to be made like his brethren in every respect'[13], 'learned obedience' – and was 'made perfect' – 'through what he suffered',[14] 'in every respect was tempted as we are',[15] and even 'offered up prayers and supplications, with loud cries and tears, to him that was able to save him from death'.[16] But when he turns to the passages in which, he admits, 'it is equally obvious that pre-existence is ascribed to him', and 'this pre-existence is manifestly...thought of in the most exalted way', he merely remarks that 'we have here another close approximation of *(sic)* the kenoticism which can be surmised to lie between the original adoptionism and the several forms of incarnationism which the New Testament documents represent'[17] – by which he means that to the 'original' story of an exclusively human person who had been raised to 'divinity' there had been added a 'prologue' which depicted his pre-existent glory, without any implications whatever regarding the utter humanity of the man who stands between this glorious prologue and the 'divine' epilogue.

Similarly, he quotes some of the sayings attributed to Jesus in John's Gospel (to which he should, of course, have

[11] Contrast C. F. D. Moule, in *The Origin of Christology* (and elsewhere), where he applies a rigidly critical approach   with which I myself do not always agree   in a much more objective way.

[12] Heb. 2:11 NEB.

[13] Heb. 2:7 R.S.V.

[14] Heb. 5:8 and 9 R.S.V.

[15] Heb. 4:15 R.S.V.

[16] Heb. 5:7 R.S.V.

[17] *Op. cit.*, pp. 36f.

added several closely comparable statements in the Synoptic Gospels) and then summarily dismisses them with the double question: 'can we imagine a true man speaking in any such fashion?' and 'could anyone. . .who finds it natural, or even possible, to regard such words as the actual words of Jesus of Nazareth be thinking of him as fully a man?'[18] But this cavalier treatment really will not do. Even on the most critical basis it is inescapable, I think, that Jesus was conscious of a relationship to the One he habitually addressed as 'Abba, my Father', which was uniquely intimate, and that he spoke and acted with an innate authority which amazed his contemporaries. Knox asserts, moreover, that 'even Paul and the writer to the Hebrews, each of whom has a motive for maintaining the full integrity of the humanity [of Jesus] which John does not have – even they cannot do so without some equivocation and compromise'; and he gives three examples of contexts in which even these two writers momentarily lapse from depicting the earthly life of Jesus as that of 'a man like other men', 'born out of, and into, humanity in the same sense every man is', 'human to the lowest depths of his conscious and subconscious life'.[20] The first of these is when St. Paul, in Phil. 2:7-8, wrote that Christ 'emptied himself, taking the form (μορφήν) of a servant, being born in the likeness (ʽομοιώματι) of men. And being found in human form (σχήματι) he humbled himself and became obedient unto death, even death on a cross'; for here Knox admits that 'we cannot easily pass by the suggestion of unreality *(sic)* conveyed in 'ομοίωμα and σχήμα'- – particularly when used in the self-same context. The second example is Rom. 8:2, where St. Paul speaks of God 'sending his own Son in the likeness (ʽομοιώματι)of sinful flesh; for here, Knox comments: 'When this passage is considered in connection with the most natural reading of Phil. 2:7-8, I believe we have to recognise the presence in Paul's thought, at least sometimes or in some connections, of

[18] *Ibid.,* p. 63.
[19] *Ibid.,* p. 53.
[20] *Ibid.,* p. 67f.

a reservation, or misgiving, as to the full genuineness of the humanity of Jesus, which is essentially incompatible with his basic conception of its function or role in God's saving act'.[21] But, while it is true that both St. Paul and the author of Hebrews strongly emphasise the humility, 'weakness' and true humanity of Jesus, is the suggestion really credible that they did not regard him as essentially the *same person* as the pre-existent Son whom God sent, 'born of a woman, born under the law, to redeem those who were under the law'? And Knox's third example is taken from Hebrews 4:15 where, after saying that 'We have not a high priest who is unable to sympathise with our weaknesses but one who in every respect has been tempted as we are', the writer adds: 'yet without sinning', or 'only without sin'. On this Knox observes:

> It is striking that in both Paul and Hebrews the impulse to draw back from saying, and fully meaning, that Christ was 'like his brethren in every respect' manifests itself at the same point. Despite the violations of the logic of their respective positions which may appear to be involved in the denial, neither writer, when it comes to the test, can bring himself to say that Jesus participated in man's sinfulness.[22]

It is clear that Knox himself finds the alleged sinlessness of Jesus a distinct problem. 'His goodness was such as apparently to leave no room for the possibility of sin', he writes:

> Here grace and truth seem perfectly united; here we see expressed the full integrity and the utter abundance of love... This character of Jesus is exhibited in the Gospels and, even more important, it belongs to the deepest and most intimate memory of the Church. Here, we cannot but affirm, was a unique human goodness, 'the highest, holiest manhood'.[23]

[21] *Ibid.*, pp. 32f.
[22] *Ibid.*, pp. 44f.
[23] *Ibid.*, p. 45.

Yet he eventually concludes that

> unless sin is to be defined in a starkly and exclusively
> voluntaristic sense and, moreover, is to be associated
> only with outward, overt actions, I should say we
> cannot make so enormous an exception in Jesus' case
> without effectively separating him from our
> humanity... Human goodness is born in a struggle
> with evil – with evil in the environing world and within
> the heart itself – and is precisely what it is on that
> account.

And he adds (rightly, but somewhat inconsequentially, I
should have thought): 'It has its characteristic excellence
and beauty only because it bears the scars of battle.[24]

Knox is certainly conscious – to some extent, at least – of
the vital significance of what he terms God's 'saving act' to
the whole subject of Christology. He emphasises, for example, that 'Paul finds the meaning of Jesus' earthly life in a
way of dealing with sin and death', for it 'was not that men
needed to be *shown* something to be saved, but rather that
something had to be *done* for them'.[25] This is finely said; but
he isolates one aspect of that atoning work of Christ when he
insists, rightly, that what had to be done for sinful men and
women was 'Something which could be done only by, or in,
or through, a man',[26] but omits to say that it was also
something which could be done only by a Saviour who was
one with God as well as one with man. Paul saw man's need,
he writes, in terms of both guilt and bondage. In the case of
guilt, 'something more, and other, than a change of heart *in
us* is required if we are to be reconciled'; while, in the case of
bondage, man 'needs rescuing. Someone must vanquish his
enemy and set him free'.[27] This, again, is very true, and is
why Paul's concept of the 'redemption which is in Christ

[24] *Ibid.,* pp. 69f.
[25] *Ibid.,* p. 80.
[26] *Ibid.*
[27] *Ibid.,* pp. 29f.

Jesus' was that God 'put him forward as an expiation (or 'propitiation') by his blood';[28] 'made him to be sin for us who knew no sin, that in him we might become the righteousness of God';[29] and 'disarmed the principalities and powers and made a public example of them, triumphing over them in him'.[30] But this would be meaningless – and flagrantly unjust – had there been no essential identity between the God who 'meant by this to demonstrate his justice' and the Christ who loved us, and 'gave himself' for us. It is precisely because of this basic identity that 'we have redemption through his blood [that is, his atoning death], the forgiveness of sins'.[31] Strangely enough, however, Knox asserts that Paul 'says nothing about repentance' and 'does not find the term "forgiveness" important and relevant in this connection'.[32]

When Knox turns to the 'New Creation' we find, once more, that he wears the same blinkers, and is still able to look in one direction only. He is perfectly clear about the continuity of the new creation with the old, for he emphasises that the idea in Paul's mind 'is not a new mankind *created,* but the old mankind *redeemed*'.[33] Similarly, he insists on the absolute necessity for Christ (as the 'second Adam' and the one who inaugurated the new creation) to have complete continuity with the race he came to redeem; but he is totally unable to envisage any corresponding – or accompanying – discontinuity. On this subject he becomes almost stridently dogmatic. 'There is no other conceivable way of being a man,' he asserts. 'Not only is it impossible, by definition, that God should become a man, it is also impossible, by definition, that he should "make" one. A true human being could not be freshly

[28] Rom. 3:25.
[29] 2 Cor. 5:21.
[30] Col. 2:15. Or the last two words might be translated 'in it' (i.e. the cross).
[31] Rom. 3:25.
[32] Cf. also Eph. 4:32; Col. 2:14; and Col. 3:13. There are, moreover, a number of other curious assertions in this very patchy book: e.g. that the statement in Heb. 7:27 that Christ 'offered up himself' does not refer to Golgotha, and that 'Christ's saving work was still to be done when he left the tomb' (*Ibid.,* p. 35).
[33] *Ibid.,* p. 82.

created. Such a creation might look like a man and even speak like a man. He might be given flesh like a man's and a man's faculties, but he would not *be* a man. He would not be a man because he would not belong to the organic human process, to the actually existing concrete entity in nature and history, which is, and alone is, *man*'.[34] I confess that I find such one-sided dogmatism much less convincing than, for example, C. F. D. Moule's careful and balanced examination of the 'paradox' of the way in which the New Testament writers depict the humanity of Jesus as 'both continuous with and discontinuous from that of the rest of mankind'. It is evident, he writes, that Jesus' humanity was, in the 'generic' sense, continuous with our humanity. But on the other side of the paradox, he insists, 'is an affirmation of a newness and sinlessness which mark a distinction between Christ's humanity and ours'.[35]

We can in part agree with Knox that

> To recognise that there are grounds. . .for speaking of 'God the Father, God the Son [or Logos], and God the Holy Ghost' as three hypostases, or personal modes of the divine being, and also that it was specifically 'God the Word' who in Christ was made flesh – to recognise all this is by no means the same thing as identifying Jesus of Nazareth with this pre-existing, and always existing, hypostasis. Just as the reality of God is not exhausted in the Logos, yet is fully present in it, so the reality of the Logos was fully present in the Event of which the human life of Jesus was the centre and therefore pre-eminently in that human life itself, but without being simply identical with Jesus.[36]

But there is a vast difference between insisting, with Temple, that we must not imagine that 'the Creative Word

---

[34] *Ibid.*, p. 67ff.
[35] 'The manhood of Jesus in the New Testament', in *Christ, Faith and History*, pp. 102ff.
[36] *Op. cit.*, pp. 109f.

was so self-emptied as to have no being except in the Infant Jesus' (and so, in *that* sense, 'cannot simply identify Jesus, for all his importance, with one of the "persons" of the Trinity', as Knox goes on to say), on the one hand, and affirming that 'the reality of the Logos' was not present – and, indeed, incarnate – in Jesus *himself,* but only in the 'Event' of which his human life was the centre. Knox even goes so far as to state that

> we must refrain from such an identification not only in speaking of the earthly life and of any conceivable pre-existence, but in speaking of his present being and status, as well. For in the resurrection his manhood was not abandoned; it was divinely exalted and transfigured. He is still the human being human hands once handled and human hearts remembered and remember still. This continuing humanity is absolutely essential to his 'Lordship'. He can be 'our Lord'. . .only because we can think of him, not only as having *once* been with us and of us but also as being with us and of us still.[37]

Some of this is profoundly true and deeply moving. But Knox continues:

> If we needed to think of him in his exaltation as being God himself, or one of the 'persons' in God[38], that belief would be as formidable an obstacle to our acceptance of the full authenticity of his manhood on earth as the doctrine of his pre-existence can be.

But here, I think, Knox is rightly insisting on the continuing humanity of the exalted Lord, but at the cost of completely denying his eternal Godhead. His criterion throughout is not what God has revealed, but whether the point at issue constitutes 'any obstacle' to the 'full authen-

[37] *Ibid.,* pp. 110f.
[38] For a discussion of this point, see 149f. and 156f. below.

ticity' of Jesus' humanity – in the extreme and exclusive sense in which, alone, he can envisage this. If it does, then a large part of the New Testament, and an essential element in the Church's faith all down the ages, must count for nothing.

Knox himself, as we have seen, has considerable sympathy with the 'adoptionism' which he believes, 'almost of necessity', to have represented the earliest Christology of the Church. Once this had been abandoned, however, there were, in his view, only two feasible alternatives: Kenoticism or Docetism. By the first of these he means the story of one who was truly divine becoming, for the duration of his earthly life, utterly and exclusively human, and then returning to his original status; and, by the second, he means that this divine being retained his full deity throughout, but at the expense of never having become truly man. This he rightly rejects as totally incompatible with the Gospels, to say nothing of the Creeds. But *as a story* he regards kenoticism as 'superb, indeed perfect'.[39] Here one is reminded of Dr. Frances Young's moving testimony, in *The Myth of God Incarnate*, that

> For me, experience of suffering, sin, decay and 'abnormality' as a constituent part of the world, would make belief in God impossible without a Calvary-centred myth...that on the cross, God in Christ entered into the suffering, the evil and the sin of his world – entered the darkness and transformed it into light, into blazing glory....

But 'if such a faith is to have any grounds whatever', she continues, 'it does appear at first sight to require the conclusion that Jesus on the cross *was God*'. So she asks herself the question 'will my myth cease to be real if I find it intellectually impossible to make the ontological equation: Jesus = God?' She knows perfectly well, of course, that this is not 'what Christian tradition has claimed', for to 'reduce

---

[39] *Ibid.*, pp. 94-97.

all of God to a human incarnation is virtually in-
conceivable'.[40] But 'the Christian', as Knox observes, 'not
only sings and prays; he also thinks';[41] and the stumbling
block, it seems, is 'the central belief of Christians' – as Brian
Hebblethwaite puts it – 'that God himself, without ceasing to
be God, has come among us, not just in but *as* a particular
man'.[42]

Again and again, however, some of the participants in
what I have termed the 'contemporary debate' assert that to
regard Jesus as both God and man, in any ontological sense,
represents a contradiction in terms. But after quoting Don
Cupitt's insistence that 'The eternal God, and a historical
man, are two beings of quite different ontological status. It is
simply unintelligible to declare them identical', and Hick's
repetition of Spinoza's dictum that talk of one who is both
God and man is like talk of a square circle, Hebblethwaite
aptly comments:

> Both writers are so convinced that a literal doctrine of
> incarnation *cannot* be true, that they try to represent
> this as a logical impossibility. Yet as soon as we
> examine these assertions, it becomes clear that no case
> whatsoever has actually been made out for the conclu-
> sion that incarnation-talk is self-contradictory. What,
> after all, is the basis for comparing talk of one who is
> both God and man to talk of a square circle? The terms
> 'square' and 'circle' are precisely defined terms, and
> their logical incompatibility is obvious from the
> definitions. But 'God' and 'man' are far from being
> such tightly defined concepts. It is difficult enough to
> suppose that we have a full and adequate grasp of what
> it is to be a human being. We certainly have no such
> grasp of the divine nature. Who are we to say that the
> essence of God is such as to rule out the possibility of
> his making himself present in the created world as a

---

[40] *The Myth of God Incarnate*, pp. 34f.
[41] *Op. cit.*, p. 98.
[42] 'Incarnation – the Essence of Christianity', in Theology (March, 1977), p. 85.

human being, while in no way ceasing to be the God he ever is? A similar point can be made in respect of Cupitt's remarks. Certainly the eternal God and a historical man are beings of different ontological status. But the claim of the Christian tradition has been that the ontology of God is such as to permit the infinite source of all created being to come amongst us as a man. Again, who are we to say that the ontological status of God is such as to render this logically impossible?[43]

For another outstanding example of what may be loosely described as the same school of thought we will turn to John Robinson's book, *The Human Face of God*.[44] As is his habit, Robinson here examines the New Testament evidence, as he sees it, with meticulous care; and, while the book is sprinkled with remarks to which exception might be taken, he expresses himself with admirable pungency and makes many excellent points. It is much more in his negative than his positive assertions – in what he denies rather than what he affirms – that he seems to me to present an inadequate view; and it is only in his last chapter, where he largely turns from the New Testament to a number of recent authors, that he leaves me, for one, bewildered and gasping. But it is with obvious sincerity that he writes, in his Preface, that 'Churchmen and professional theologians who know what they are looking for will be ready with their stickers to label my position "reductionist", "adoptionist", "humanist" and the rest. I believe in fact that they will be wrong and that it is none of these things. For I fully share their concerns – yet doubt if these can be matched by the old orthodoxies.' His own concern 'is to a large extent with self-questioning – with *how today* one can truthfully and meaningfully say (in the words of the earliest and shortest confession), "Jesus is Lord." I shall be writing as one who *wants* to make that confession.'[45]

---

[43] *Op. cit.*, p. 86.
[44] SCM Press, London, 1973.
[45] Cf. pp. viii and xi.

There can be no doubt, moreover, that Robinson goes much further than Hick in the position he gives to Christ. He states explicitly, for example, that what he pleads for 'is the highest possible Christology in relation *both* to the humanity *and* to the divinity of Christ'.[46] His desire is 'to affirm Jesus as the Son of God as the New Testament speaks of him, as the one who was called at his baptism and vindicated at his resurrection to *be* God's decisive word to men, the embodiment of his nature and the enactment of his will. The sole question is how to express this identity of the divine with the human. 'Is it effected by God's joining a second (human) nature to his own', he asks, 'or is it by his using, acting through, a man? Is it, in a phrase, by taking manhood or by taking a man?'[47] He is himself persuaded that 'there is no other of whom it can be said that to have seen him is to have seen the Father';[48] and, while 'God dwells in different men in different degrees. . .the decisive difference in Christ's case is that it was "as in a son", and that the indwelling was by personal union and not just by intermittent grace.'[49] As might be expected from two more recent books,[50] moreover, he is far more positive than Hick on the subject of the historicity of the picture we get of Jesus in the Gospels; for he asserts that 'the time is over-ripe for counter-attacks against some of the absurdities that are allowed to pass for critical conclusions.'[51]

Although, in his view, the 'old securities in history on which Christology was based. . .have been undermined beyond repair', he does not believe 'that this need lead to scepticism or cynicism – or to a flight from the Jesus of history as unattainable or unnecessary'.[52] We must not, of course, 'make the judgment of faith reducible to human knowledge'; but he asserts that it is 'inescapable for any

[46] *Op. cit.*, p. 141.
[47] *Op. cit.*, p. 197.
[48] *Op. cit.*, p. 227.
[49] *Op. cit.*, p. 205.
[50] *Redating the New Testament* and *Can we trust the New Testament?*
[51] *Op. cit.*, p. 28.
[52] *The Human Face of God*, p. 31.

historical religion such as Christianity' that 'the judgment of faith is dependent on, in the sense of being vulnerable to, the facts of history'.[53]

In regard to the resurrection, again, he goes much further than Hick, Lampe or many others, for he argues that 'if the so-called "appearances" had been purely subjective hallucinations. . .or purely private, it is incredible that Paul and others could have rested so much on them – especially when he sits so lightly to his own visions.'[54] What, then, of the empty tomb?

> Again, the credibility gap seems to me to rule out deliberate deceit by the disciples or that the women went to the wrong tomb and no one bothered to check, or that Jesus never really died, or that his body was not buried but thrown into a lime-pit (the burial is one of the earliest and best-attested facts about Jesus, being recorded in 1 Corinthians as well as in all four Gospels. . .). More plausible is the oft-repeated thesis that the subsequent belief in the resurrection *created* the empty tomb story because this is what the Jewish hope would have pointed to. But what it pointed to was a rising at the last day for final judgment. Prior to that, the most that could have been expected would have been either a temporary resuscitation (like that of Jairus' daughter) or a return in spirit (e.g. of Elijah and, perhaps, of "John the Baptist raised from the dead"), with neither of which is the noun "resurrection" ever associated. *No one* expected to find a grave empty in the middle of history.[55]

The evidence, he asserts, suggests that the story of the tomb represents 'very early tradition', and he quotes Bornhäuser's remark that 'it should never have come to the point that in spite of the *etaphē*, "he was buried", of 1 Cor.

---

[53] *Op. cit.,* p. 126.
[54] *Op. cit.,* pp. 129f.
[55] *Ibid.,* pp. 131f.

15:3 f. the phrase "he was raised again the third day" was understood in any other way than as a raising from the tomb'.[56] Then, after further discussion, he sums up his own view by saying that the evidence suggests 'that, while the finding of the grave empty was not invented by the early church, it neither created belief in the resurrection nor was created by it. It was simply part of what was indelibly remembered to have happened. *Why* it was empty admits historically of no certain explanation'.[57]

Robinson makes much of the distinction, suggested by Professor Maurice Wiles, between two 'stories' about the Incarnation, redemption, and much else: on the one hand a 'natural, scientific, descriptive' story, and on the other a 'supernatural, mythological and interpretative story'. 'We have learnt,' he writes, 'to see the natural and the supernatural not as two layers of being that have been joined together, so much as two sets of language, man-language and God-language, in which it is possible to speak of a single cosmic process'.[58] So, in regard to Jesus, 'it is not that one is true *or* the other, or that one is real at the expense of the other'.[59] Yet, if there was not an *adequate* basis in the *human* story, then 'it would be difficult, if not impossible, to sustain the judgment of faith that in this man took place the decisive act of God in history'.[60]

On the one side, therefore, Robinson insists, again and again, that Jesus was completely one of us: *totus in nostris*. 'Today, the slightest suggestion that he was not, in the words of the Chalcedonian Definition, 'completely human *(teleion en anthrōpotēti)*. . .of one substance with us *(homoousion hēmin)* as regards his manhood' is, he asserts, 'much more destructive of the Gospel than doubts about his divinity';[61] and he makes great play of the fantastically docetic views of many of the Alexandrian divines – such as

---

[56] Cf. *ibid.*, p. 133.
[57] *Ibid.*, p. 135.
[58] *Ibid.*, pp. 116f.
[59] *Ibid.*, p. 171.
[60] *Ibid.*, p. 125.
[61] *Ibid.*, p. 38.

the statement of Clement that 'it would be ridiculous to imagine that the body of the Redeemer, in order to exist, had the usual needs of man'; that of Athanasius that 'the Word disguised himself by appearing in a body'; of Cyril that 'he permitted his own flesh to weep a little, although it was in its nature tearless and incapable of grief'; or of Hilary that 'when he ate and drank, it was a concession, not to his own necessities, but to our habits'.[62] Similarly, he quotes D. M. Baillie's statement that it is 'nonsense to say that "He is Man" unless we mean that He is a man'.[63] It is not enough to affirm with Justin Martyr that Jesus 'had the body and soul and spirit of a man', for Robinson maintains that 'this is to ignore completely what for us is a *sine qua non* of personal existence, namely, the nexus of biological, historical and social relationships with our fellow-men and the universe as a whole. If that is not there, then Jesus may have entered completely into the place where we are – but only as a visitor. He was like one of us, but he was not one of us.'[64]

It is precisely at this point that he becomes, in my view, exceedingly doctrinaire. If Jesus 'entered completely into the place where we were', and was genuinely 'like one of us', does that not satisfy the reference in Hebrews to the fact that 'he had to be made like these brothers of his in every way', while still making it possible to assert his deity in a deeper sense than is possible from Robinson's view-point? Instead, he pours ridicule on the concept of a 'divine being arriving to look like a man', 'a celestial figure lowering himself to become a man', or even a 'sort of centaur or batman'.[65] The point to which he continually returns is that 'to assert incarnation' is to insist that Jesus had 'all the pre-history of man in his genes'; that 'the influence not only of his environment but of his heredity must be pressed to the full'; that he must 'have belonged to one particular blood-group' and to have 'had the characteristics of one psychological type

[62] *Ibid.,* pp. 39f.
[63] See pp. 145f. below.
[64] *Ibid.,* pp. 40f.
[65] *Ibid.,* pp. 161f., 166 and 115.

rather than another'.[66] We can certainly agree with him that
it is manifestly ridiculous to suggest, as some have, that
Jesus excelled all other men in every sphere – beauty of
form, perfection of health, and skill as 'dialectician,
philosopher, mathematician, doctor, politician, orator' or
anything else;[67] indeed, the prophet wrote of him that 'he
had no beauty, no majesty to draw our eyes, no grace to
make us delight in him'. But the fact that he was son of Mary
was enough to ensure that he had human genes – although
to be *male* without a human father would certainly have
involved a break of some sort with the natural order[68]
(which is what the New Testament specifically records). And
it may be observed in passing, in this context, that Robinson
is careful to insist that 'to say that "science"
has disproved the virgin birth or that physical miracles of
this sort are impossible. . .would be totally unwarranted
dogmatism', and 'nothing I have said should be taken to
mean that I am dogmatically excluding the possibility of
virgin birth. . .or indeed any radical discontinuity or novelty
in the historical process' – although he does in fact occasionally lapse into assuming that Jesus had a human
father.[69] What Robinson is almost obsessively anxious to do
is 'to take seriously the requirement (which no one
theoretically would dispute) that if Jesus Christ is to be
anything for us at all he must have been genuinely a man,
with the peculiarities and limitations of one unique individual'. But there is, he says, a wide-spread 'reluctance to
press this to the limit, and this reluctance is connected with
the desire. . .to see in him more than a man – and to admit
nothing that might prejudice that "more".'[70]

Yet Robinson himself is quite clear that Jesus' words and
works were 'not simply those of any man faithful and open
to God but the self-expression of God acting in him and

[66] *Ibid.*, pp. 42ff. and 69.
[67] *Ibid.*, p. 71.
[68] Since natural parthenogenesis among humans, if it occurred, would produce a female child.
[69] *Ibid.*, pp. 51, 138 and 171.
[70] *Op. cit.*, p. 67.

through him'. Jesus claims that he, and he alone, has 'seen the Father'; and John unhesitatingly declares that

> As 'the only son', or even 'the only one, who is himself God', he alone has 'made him known.' Again, 'no one ever went up into heaven except the one who came down from heaven, the Son of Man'; and it is this Son of Man alone who can give and sustain eternal life. Jesus is and Jesus does what no other man can be or do.

Yet Robinson maintains that 'in order to be this and do this, he is not other than a man in complete continuity with all other men.'[71] What is inescapable is that in the authority with which he refers to the law, in forgiving sins and in quelling the spirits and the powers of nature, Jesus

> steps, in the eyes of his contemporaries, into the space reserved for God. . . He says that men's attitude to him will decide God's attitude to them. In his parables he justifies his conduct by the way *God* acts. Indeed, he is there to be 'the parable of God'.[72]

More than this, however, Robinson will not concede, because how could Jesus be genuinely a man, he asks, 'if all the time "underneath", as it were, he was really God?'

When he turns to specific problems Robinson is sometimes decisive and clear-cut and at others seems to indulge his penchant for 'both. . .and' rather than 'either. . .or'. 'As soon as Jesus Christ was, or could be, represented as a pre-existent being who had come down from heaven', he writes, 'then the genuineness of his humanity while he was on earth was open to question'; so he explains his pre-existence as a 'translated' form of fore-ordination.[73] He is himself, it seems, perfectly prepared to accept a doctrine of incarnation under which 'a life, power

---

[71] *Op. cit.*, pp. 113 and 174f.
[72] *Op. cit.*, pp. 192f.
[73] *Op. cit.*, p. 37.

or activity. . .which is not as such a person comes to embodiment and expression (whether partial or total) in an individual human being'.[74] What he strenuously denies is the concept of pre-existence 'which became explicit in the doctrine of *anhypostasia*' and 'meant the prior existence in heaven of an individual *hypostasis* or *persona* who was in the fullness of time to become the subject of the human nature taken from the virgin Mary'. On this view

> the Logos was already in the fullest sense a person (of the Trinity). At the Incarnation, he did not become an individual; he became human – without, of course, ceasing to be divine. He was *a* being, who did not start like us but was *made like* us by sharing our life.

It is this concept, he declares, 'which it is so difficult (if not impossible) to combine with Jesus being, with the rest of us, a genuine product of the evolutionary process.'[75] But the Epistle to the Hebrews states specifically that 'in this the final age [God] has spoken to us in the Son . . . through whom he created all orders of existence'; and that, to redeem us, he had to share our flesh and blood, 'to be made like us in every respect', and 'taste death for every man'. There is no reason that I can see, however, why we should equate the divine Logos or Son so *completely* with Jesus, or Jesus with the Second Person of the Trinity, as to suggest that *Jesus as Jesus* was pre-existent, or that the Logos was altogether confined to the person of Jesus during his earthly life.[76] But Robinson is so absolutely insistent that Jesus *must* be 'a genuine product of the evolutionary process' that this criterion (in what appears to be an essentially inflated form) dominates his whole Christology. Thus he argues that the statements in Galatians 4:4 that 'God sent his own Son, born of a woman, born under the law', and in Romans 8:3 that 'What the law could never do . . . God has done; by sending his own Son in a

---

[74] *Op. cit.*, pp. 103 and 147f.
[75] *Op. cit.*, p. 148.
[76] Or, possibly, even today. Cf, pp. 134, 147-150, 156f.

form like that of our own sinful nature . . .' do *not* portray 'a divine being arriving to look like a man' (which is true), but 'a man born like the rest of us, from within the nexus of the flesh, law and sin, who nevertheless embodied the divine initiative and saving presence so completely that he was declared at his baptism and confirmed at his resurrection to be everything God himself was' (which seems to me a comment which is dangerously close to 'private interpretation'!).[77] And examples of this sort of thing recur again and again.

But Robinson goes much further than Knox in exposing the inadequacy of adoptionism. The term *homoousios,* inserted in the Nicene Creed 'to rule out the Arian belief in a Christ who was *neither* fully human *nor* fully divine but a sort of angelic compromise', was 'retained in the Chalcedonian Definition against those "who shamelessly pretend that he who was born of the holy Mary was a *mere* man"'; for the Cyrilline school 'had a tendency to smell out denial of divinity (a man *and nothing else*) whenever insistence was laid on the fact that Jesus was *completely* human, like everyone else'. This reaction, he says, is not dead yet. [Indeed, he thinks I am myself guilty of it.]

> Nevertheless, the reaffirmation of divine substance in Jesus stood against the view that he was just a God-like man, who speaks to us only of man and man's God-consciousness. For on this view there is no identity with the divine action: Jesus is not God at work, God is not implicated in what he says and does. The *homoouios* was there to assert the *vere deus.*

But this Robinson himself 'has no concern to deny' – and he insists that their opponents could not understand that 'men like Theodore and Nestorius really were arguing (as we can now see) for a genuine and deeply *personal* union of God and man in Christ.'[78]

It seems to me that a particular weakness in Robinson's

---

[77] *Op. cit.,* pp. 158-162, etc.
[78] *Ibid.,* pp. 196-199.

view and presentation is in regard to the exaltation of Christ. Jesus, he insists, 'was as completely one of us as any other physical descendant of Abraham', although 'the entire fullness of God was enabled by divine grace and human obedience to find embodiment in him' – and he asserts (very questionably, I think) that 'Paul makes it abundantly clear. . .that the Incarnation meant the complete identification of God in Christ with our earthly humanity of powerless, *sinful* flesh'.[79] What, then, did in fact happen when God 'highly exalted him and graciously bestowed on him *(echarisato)* the name above every name', so that 'henceforth the human name Jesus should be inseparably linked, at its every mention in worship, with the divine name, *kyrios,* Lord'[80] – and whom, precisely, are we worshipping, and sometimes addressing in prayer? Is it in any real sense Jesus himself, or God *in* one who always has been, is still and always will be, essentially, and only, human? Robinson would reply, it seems, that Jesus was, and is, 'the complete plenipotentiary of God';[81] that he spoke and acted for God, although himself 'not a divine or semi-divine being' but 'a human figure raised up from among his brothers to be the instrument of God's decisive work and to stand in a relationship to him to which no other man is called';[82] that he was, and is, 'the very "exegesis" of the Father (John 1:18), and indeed himself *theos* (John 1:1 and 18), because *as a man* he is utterly transparent to *another*';[83] that, while he was 'totally human and therefore as independent of God as any other man, his whole life – and all that leads up to it and flows from it – is seen as the climax and fulfilment of a divine process going back to the beginning';[84] that he is 'the embodiment, the realisation of God' in a particular man, 'immanent' in the whole human process 'yet

---

[79] *Ibid.,* pp. 166f. My italics.
[80] *Ibid.*
[81] *Ibid.,* p. 155.
[82] *Ibid.,* p. 184.
[83] *Ibid.,* pp. 189f.
[84] *Ibid.,* p. 201. But I would question Robinson's attribution of this view to 'the biblical writers'.

constantly transcending it', a 'breakthrough of cosmic consciousness',[85] a human life in which God was 'reflected, defined and focussed "as in a son";[86] that 'though fully man and in no sense "more than a man", [he] is not to be confused with other men';[87] and that 'the uniqueness of Jesus was the absolute uniqueness of what God did in him'.[88] But this hotchpotch of quotations provides no real answer to the question 'Whom are we worshipping?'

In the light of this distinctly equivocal assessment, it is not surprising that Robinson, after referring to the 'discussion as to whether Jesus should properly be called unique in degree or kind', affirms that 'if one had to choose, I should side with those who opt for a "degree Christology" – however enormous the degree'.[89] Like Knox and Pittenger, moreover, he leaves us in no doubt about the criterion he applies, for he adds that 'to speak of Jesus as different in kind from all other men is to threaten, if not to destroy, his *total solidarity* with all other men, which *we have regarded as unexpendable*.'[90] I suppose, moreover, that this is – in part – the reason why he speaks of the 'myth' of

the eternal humanity of Christ, the mediator, who ever lives to make intercession for us. Demythologised, this myth of the heavenly world stands for the fact that, spiritually speaking, the representation of God continues. The incognito by which he must be represented by man is not abrogated. What the exaltation does is not to cancel the *kenōsis*: it seals the process of identification as the way of God's coming to his identity in men and men in God, which is the Kingdom.[91]

---

[85] *Ibid.,* pp. 203f.
[86] *Ibid.,* p. 209.
[87] *Ibid.,* p. 210, quoting Van Buren.
[88] *Ibid.,* p. 211.
[89] *Ibid.,* pp. 209f.
[90] *Ibid.,* p. 210. My italics.
[91] *Ibid.,* p. 215. But see pp. 149f. and 156f. below.

For myself, however, I much prefer the doctrine in its original and pre-demythologised, form.

Not surprisingly, Robinson's Christology provides no basis for any adequate doctrine of the Atonement. Indeed, he objects to

> the way in which Christian theology has come to use the definite article, combined with a capital letter, in such phrases as 'the Atonement', 'the Resurrection', 'the Parousia'. This is, by intention, a way of seeking to assert universality, finality – the element of the once and for all.

But this, he believes, suffers from the fatal defect of 'defining Christ out of universal common experience'. So, he says:

> If I am asked 'Do you believe in the Atonement?' or 'the Resurrection' or 'the Parousia', the questioner expects to elicit my attitude to something Jesus is supposed to have done on the cross, something that is alleged to have happened 'on the third day' or something that may happen at the end of the world.[92]

With this last statement I would fully agree – except that I would omit the words 'supposed', 'alleged' and 'may'. To leave out the definite article, as Robinson would prefer, and ask instead 'Do you believe in atonement?', 'Do you believe in resurrection?', 'Do you believe in parousia (presence, or coming)?' may, indeed, be an excellent way of starting a conversation and eliciting a meaningful response; but when Robinson asserts that

> the 'the' of the traditional Christian myth removes the reality of Christ from the kind of present where every eye might in fact see him to a distant past or to the

[92] *Ibid.,* pp. 230f.

remote future or to 'the divine superworld' where Christ lives in a timeless realm, as unrelated to the continuing course of events as was his pre-existence to the earlier biological process.[93]

about this I can only say that I see the matter from what seems to be a diametrically opposite point of view. It is precisely because of what Jesus did do on the cross that I have a present, living experience of forgiveness; because of what did in fact happen 'on the third day' that I know him as a living Saviour now; and because I believe he is coming again one day that, instead of thinking in terms of some 'divine superworld' and 'timeless realm', I have a certain sense (although not nearly as vivid as I would wish) of imminence and urgency.

[93] *Ibid.*

5
Some Examples of the Contemporary Debate II

IN MY LAST CHAPTER I ATTEMPTED TO SUMMARISE, AND in part to discuss, the christological views of two reasonably representative participants in what I have termed 'the contemporary debate': Professor John Knox and Dr. John Robinson. Both of them take as their fundamental – and even 'unexpendable' – criterion the assertion that Jesus, in himself, was not only truly but exclusively human, a 'man like other men'.[1] It is absolutely impossible, they insist, for God to become a man, or even to 'make' a man[2]; for to be part of the human race is not only to look, act, feel and think like a man, but to *be* a man at the very centre and core of one's being. Granted this basic postulate, however, both of them are prepared – and, indeed, eager – to go a long way in regard to the status they accord to Jesus. The risen Lord, Knox affirms, is both human and divine: '*divinely* human'.[3] God had assuredly acted in him in a unique way which makes even his human life 'different from all others'.[4] Similarly, in Robinson's view, Jesus was 'the self-expressive activity of God',[5] 'the very "exegesis" of the Father',[6] the one who '*is* God to us and for us'.[7] 'The uniqueness of Jesus', he asserts, 'was the absolute uniqueness of what God did in him.'[8] For both theologians, it is clear, the sticking point is not primarily the functional but the ontological; for they

---

[1] Knox, *Humanity and Divinity of Christ*, p. 63.
[2] *Ibid.*, p. 67.
[3] *Ibid.*, p. 54.
[4] *Ibid.*, p. 113.
[5] *The Human Face of God*, p. 104.
[6] *Ibid.*, p. 189.
[7] *Ibid.*, p. 114.
[8] *Ibid.*, p. 211.

both believe that God acted in the 'Christ-event', or even in Jesus himself, in a uniquely revelatory and even 'redemptive' way – although the precise sense in which they use the latter term is far from clear. But their Christology, as I see it, does not really entitle us to *worship* the risen Christ, or to address him in prayer; and it certainly does not provide a basis for any objective doctrine of the Atonement. Both of them would, without doubt, confess that 'Jesus is Lord'; but for them this would not mean that he was, or is, in himself 'truly God'.

But there are a number of other participants in the contemporary debate who are more radical than Knox or Robinson, and who express their views in a much less guarded and qualified way. Some of the contributors to *The Myth of God Incarnate,* for example, are far more negative in their assessment of the evidence for the resurrection (and, of course, of much else in the Gospel records), and much more positive in their dissent from traditional christological and trinitarian doctrines. Dr. D. N. Nineham, for instance, sums up the question posed by Professor Maurice Wiles – rather more crudely than the latter, I fancy, would himself have phrased it – as:

> shall the Christian myth or story of the future be a story primarily about God or shall it, if I may put it so without irreverence, be a story which co-stars Jesus and God? Shall it be a story in which Jesus shares the leading role and has a unique or perfect status of some sort assigned to him? Or shall it be a story in which the protagonist's role belongs undividedly to God, though of course the story would tell how once he worked in a vitally important way – though not a way *necessarily* in principle unique – through the man Jesus to bring the Christian people into a relationship of reconciliation and oneness with himself?

In a situation of galloping cultural change, which has brought the doctrine of the literal divinity of Jesus into question, is it any longer worthwhile to attempt to trace the Christian's ever changing understanding of his relationship with God directly back to some identifiable element in the life, character and activity of Jesus of Nazareth?[9]

It is not my purpose to try to determine how far the other contributors to *The Myth* would go along with Dennis Nineham's statement, or what answer they would give to the question he poses. Interestingly enough, however, Professor Wiles, in his introductory essay, faces up to a problem to which I have referred more than once when he asks whether a 'Christianity without incarnation' would not 'imply that the worship of Christ, traditional throughout the whole of Christian history, was idolatrous in character'? To this he replies that

It is important to remember that in the strictest sense it is never simply Jesus who saves nor is Christ by himself the object of man's worship. Jesus as Second Person of the Trinity incarnate is the one through whom we come to the trinitarian God, the one through whom the whole Trinity acts towards us.[10]

This is no doubt true, but does not really answer the question. Is it, or is it not, right to *include* 'the Lord Jesus' in our worship, or to address him specifically, on occasion, in our prayers? For himself, Wiles had already declared, in his essay in *Christian Believing,* that he could not 'with integrity say that I believe God to be one in three persons. My questioning – historical and philosophical – does not leave me with sufficient grounds to form a belief on such a question one way or the other'[11]; while his remark in *The*

[9] *Op. cit.,* p. 202.
[10] *Ibid.,* p. 8.
[11] SPCK, London 1976, p. 126.

Remaking of Christian Doctrine[12] about 'giving a special evaluation to Jesus himself of the unique kind that Christian orthodoxy has in fact given' prompts Mascall to comment:

> Thus it appears that belief in Jesus as God incarnate is tolerable, although it goes against the basic tenet of Wiles's particular form of deism. But it is not necessary and it is, in Wiles's opinion, improbable. This must be the first form of Christianity in which the deity of Jesus is looked upon as optional; in less sophisticated ages it was either the ultimate truth that gave meaning to life or else downright idolatrous blasphemy.[13]

In his essay on 'Christianity without Incarnation?' in *The Myth*, moreover, Wiles argues that, even in the 'absence of incarnational belief', it

> would still be possible to see Jesus not only as one who embodies a full response of man to God but also as one who expresses and embodies the way of God towards men. . . For Jesus was not merely a teacher about God; the power of God was set at work in the world in a new way through his life, ministry, death and resurrection. On such a basis it is reasonable to suggest that the stories about Jesus and the figure of Jesus himself could remain a personal focus of the transforming power of God in the world.[14]

Personally, I have no doubt whatever that 'Jesus himself', as Saviour, Lord and God – and, indeed, those stories about him on which our knowledge of his earthly life is based – will still inspire Christian worship and remain the centre of Christian experience long after the arguments for the abandonment of 'ideas that are associated with "incarnation"...as a metaphysical claim about the person of

[12] CUP, Cambridge, 1967. Cf., in particular, p. 54.
[13] *Theology and the Gospel of Christ* (SPCK, London 1977), p. 40.
[14] p. 8.

Jesus' (for which Wiles sees 'a strong case')[15] have been dismissed as mere aberrations.

What united the very diverse contributors to this book is, we are told, their conviction 'that another major theological development is called for in this last part of the twentieth century': namely, 'a recognition that Jesus was (as he is presented in Acts 2:21) "a man approved by God" for a special role within the divine purpose, and that the later conception of him as God incarnate. . .is a mythological or poetic way of expressing his significance for us.'[16] But in point of fact numerous statements which couple his name with that of God, and ascribe to him a status and functions that can only be described as divine, are included in the earliest New Testament documents which have come down to us. They were written, moreover, by a former Pharisee, not a Gentile convert or a mystic devotee; and they were clearly intended to express theological convictions, not flights of poetic imagination. As Moule puts it:

> Whatever obscurities meet the investigator, it is credulous to think that Christian doctrine can be explained away as due to an evolutionary process of pious fantasy and borrowing from other cults, or that the painful dilemma that led to the use of the term incarnation can be resolved by hacking at it with an uncritical knife.[17]

It may, of course, be replied that some of the scholars concerned are highly critical in their approach: so much so that Dennis Nineham recently stated that 'so far as the real Jesus can be discerned. . .there is no reason to think that the outlook of the historical Jesus will have been such as to be any more immediately acceptable today than that of, say, the historical Paul – and, indeed, that 'no scholar today supposes that New Testament Christianity as it stands is a

[15] *Ibid.*, p. 9.
[16] *Ibid.*, p. ix.
[17] 'Incarnation: paradox that will not go away', in *The Times Higher Education Supplement*, 23 December, 1977.

possible religion for modern western man, or that the character, conduct and beliefs of Jesus, even if we knew far more about them than we do, could constitute as they stand the content of a modern faith.'[18] It is, of course, far from easy to know what, precisely, Nineham means by this somewhat arrogant statement. To qualify the 'character, conduct and beliefs of Jesus', first by the caveat 'even if we knew far more about them than we do', and then by the apparently contradictory phrase 'as they stand', seems to imply that his own thinking was less lucid than usual at this point – unless, of course, he means that Jesus' character, conduct and beliefs would not provide the total 'content' of a faith, whether ancient or modern, if isolated from their proper background, setting and explanation. But his comprehensive reference to 'New Testament Christianity' seems to exclude any such interpretation; and the more natural meaning of his words would be that the 'content' of 'a possible religion for modern western man' would have to sit very loosely indeed by any authoritative basis in the teaching or experience of the apostolic Church.

Rather than pursue this subject any further, however, it would be more profitable, I believe, to examine the 'Spirit Christology' which Professor Geoffrey Lampe has been advocating, and developing, for some years. Lampe is much warmer and more positive in his approach than are most of the contributors to *The Myth of God Incarnate,* and more ruthlessly logical and consistent than either Knox or Robinson; but it would, I think, be fair to say that his Christology rests on the same fundamental postulate – that Jesus was, in himself, totally and exclusively a man in whom the Spirit of God worked in a decisive way. He expounded this thesis in his essay on 'The Holy Spirit and the person of Christ' in 1972;[19] he developed it somewhat further in 'The Essence of Christianity: A Personal View' in 1976;[20] and he has given it

---

[18] In his Ethel M. Wood Lecture on 'New Testament Interpretation in an Historical Age' (Athlone Press, London, 1976), pp. 14f.
[19] In *Christ, Faith and History.*
[20] In *The Expository Times,* LXXVII, Feb. 1976, pp. 132ff.

full expression in his Bampton Lectures in 1976.[21] As always, Lampe writes with limpid lucidity; so his 'Spirit Christology' provides an almost ideal criterion about which to ask two questions: the first, raised by Dennis Nineham in the Epilogue to *The Myth of God Incarnate,* can be summarised by asking whether this view will really stand up to critical challenge, while the second, posed by Lampe himself at the end of his essay on 'The Holy Spirit and the person of Christ', is whether this view gives adequate expression to Christian experience, or must Spirit Christology after all give way to the doctrine of the Incarnation?

'There are two affirmations', Lampe insists in *God as Spirit,*

> which in their different ways sum up the attitude of Christians towards the person of Jesus. One comes from the first century: 'Jesus is Lord'. The other is contemporary, and was often seen on car-stickers a few years ago: 'Jesus is alive today'. Neither of these affirmations gives an analytic account of Christology. Taken together, however, they raise the Christological problem in two of its aspects, for 'Jesus is Lord' prompts the question, 'How, then, is Jesus related to the Lord God?', and 'Jesus is alive today' compels us to ask how Jesus is related to believers here and now. They also lead us to ask a third question, 'How is God's relationship to men before and apart from Jesus to be understood in the light of the relationship of Jesus both to God and also to ourselves as present day believers?'[22]

The affirmation 'Jesus is Lord', he says, 'expresses the conviction that Jesus uniquely mediates the authority of God' and 'transcends the category of ordinary humanity'. But at an exceedingly early date this belief 'had already been carried a stage further' and 'Jesus does not only act as the agent of God's rule' but is actually identified with the Lord

---

[21] Published under the title *God as Spirit* (Clarendon Press, Oxford, 1977).
[22] *God as Spirit,* pp. 1f.

God of whom it had been written: 'I have given a promise. . .that will not be broken, that to me every knee shall bend'. Conversely, 'Jesus is Lord' affirms that the Lord God of the Old Testament 'is in some mysterious way identical with Jesus the Galilean teacher.' So

> The task of Christology is to explore that mysterious way and to offer an interpretation of Jesus which can adequately explain this two-way affirmation that Jesus is Lord without denying either that our experience of God is focussed upon, and articulated by reference to, the historical human person, Jesus, or that in the historical human Jesus we encounter no less than the Lord God of our present experience.

And the slogan 'Jesus is alive today' raises 'the same Christological question with particular reference to its second aspect: "What is the relationship of the Jesus described in the Gospels to Christians here and now?" What does it mean to assert that Jesus is alive now? It obviously does not mean that the first-century Jew from Nazareth is alive in the way in which we ourselves are alive today. We do not see him, recognise him, speak to him, listen to his voice.'[23]

Lampe goes on to say that it is true that 'many people do in fact claim to meet him' (and, we might add, not only speak to the risen Christ but hear his voice speaking to them through the Gospel records). But Lampe asserts that

> Those who talk of meeting and speaking to Jesus would find it hard to explain the difference between that experience and encountering, or being encountered by, God; and in fact I think the latter is what they actually mean: they are experiencing God who was in Jesus, God who is, therefore, recognised by reference to the revelatory experience recorded in the New Testament and reflected upon in the whole subsequent Christian tradition.[24]

[23] *Ibid.*, p. 2.
[24] *Ibid.*, pp. 2f.

Frankly, however, I do not think that this gloss is good enough. No one who believes in the essential unity of the Godhead makes any sharp distinction, of course, between God and Christ; but I have no doubt whatever that when I direct my prayers specifically to 'the Lord Jesus' I am addressing the One who walked the hills of Galilee and the streets of Jerusalem, who 'bore my sins in his body on the tree', and who is now exalted 'to the right hand of God' and actually 'interceding' for me. If, moreover, a Christian's experience of 'meeting and speaking to Jesus' is in fact indistinguishable from encountering, or being encountered by, the God who was only 'inspirationally' present in Jesus, I cannot see why a Jew should not, in principle, make a similar claim about Moses, Elijah or any of the prophets who were inspired by the same God – to revert to the third christological question which Lampe posed at the beginning of his book.[25] To Lampe himself, I know, God is 'for ever God-disclosed-in-Jesus', and he cannot picture God except in 'Jesus terms'. With this moving confession of faith[26] I profoundly concur; but I must confess that I cannot really understand how, on his hypothesis, he can explain and defend what he terms the 'central conviction of all Christians. . . that Christ is the focal point of the continuing encounter between God and man throughout human history', or how he is himself 'justified in assigning this central and decisive significance to Jesus Christ'.[27] Yet the Gospel record of the Transfiguration clearly demonstrates that the apostolic Church made a sharp distinction between Jesus and either Moses or Elijah – a distinction epitomised in the voice that declared 'This is my Son, my Beloved; listen to him.'[28]

There were many factors in this clear cut distinction – a distinction, I believe, not only of degree but of kind.[29] There

[25] Cf. p. 114 above.
[26] Quoted (with permission) from a personal letter.
[27] *Ibid.*, pp. 13 and 96.
[28] Mark 9:7.
[29] *Pace* Lampe, in *Christ, Faith and History*, p. 126; and 'The Essence of Christianity', p. 133.

can be no doubt, however, that it was primarily the resurrection, and subsequent exaltation, which prompted the disciples instinctively to regard Jesus as Lord, and to begin to identify him with Yahweh. Lampe himself recognised this when he started his essay on 'The Holy Spirit and the person of Christ' by affirming that 'The resurrection is the starting-point for Christology. The first Christians were convinced that "the Jesus we speak of has been raised by God", and that "God has made this Jesus. . .both Lord and Messiah" (Acts 2:32, 36)'. It was this, he insisted, that made them seek 'an interpretation of his person. . .which would justify the worship of a man who had been crucified.' In *God as Spirit*, moreover, he devotes much space to the resurrection; but it is significant that his whole approach has changed radically since he engaged in a discussion of this subject with Professor Donald MacKinnon in 1968.[30] At that time he argued strongly, it is true, against 'a fully corporeal presence of Jesus after his death', and also (though less emphatically) against the belief 'that the physical body of Jesus had been transformed in the grave into a spiritual body, and that it was no longer there at Easter because it had been changed into another substance which did not exist spatially.'[31] But it is clear that on this point he allowed the 'finely balanced' scales of the historical evidence to be weighed down by his theological conviction that Christ's resurrection was not – and *must* not have been – 'different in kind from what we may hope for through him'; so he insisted that if his body 'was raised physically from the grave and did not see corruption, or if his body was transformed after death into something different. . .then he did not experience the whole of our human destiny.'[32] In regard to the resurrection appearances, however, he was at that time prepared to

[30] Published by Mowbrays, London, under the title *The Resurrection*.

[31] *Op. cit.*, p. 46. Lampe admitted that it is possible that this was what St. Paul himself believed, but thought it 'improbable'. But it seems to me that on this point the weight of evidence is overwhelmingly against him. Cf. pp. 71f. above and G. B. Caird, *Saint Luke* (Pelican, London, 1963), p. 255.

[32] *Ibid.*, pp. 18 and 58f. Cf. also p. 97. But although I do not at all agree with him about this, it is not directly relevant to the Incarnation as such.

argue, equally strongly, that the disciples had had objective encounters with the risen Christ. 'Unless something extraordinary happened to convince them that against all their expectation God had reversed his apparent verdict on Jesus', he insisted, 'I cannot imagine that they would later on have taken immense risks to assert in public that a man who had been condemned and hanged was no less than God's Messiah'.[33] He conceded, of course, that the assertion that

> Jesus was raised by God and exalted as the Lord of glory is not a statement which the historian *as such* has any grounds either for affirming or denying. It lies outside his province. It is an assertion that is possible only to faith. But faith makes this assertion *on the basis of certain things which are recorded as having actually happened at Easter.* The claims which Christian faith makes are an interpretation which it puts upon these happenings.[34]

But in 1966 he was himself prepared unequivocally to affirm that

> Professor MacKinnon and I agree in the belief that the Resurrection was an event in the external world: that Jesus was actually raised from the dead. In holding this belief we differ from some recent writers on the subject of Easter. They maintain that Jesus 'rose' in so far as his followers came to understand his true significance. My sermon, on the other hand, asserted in the strongest possible terms that the Resurrection was a fact . . . Like Professor MacKinnon in his Easter meditation, I based my sermon on the assumption that there was an objective Easter event, and that it was this event which produced the dramatic change in the outlook of the disciples; that to speak of 'Easter' is not a way of describing the disciples' growing conviction that Jesus

---

[33] *Ibid.,* pp. 30f.
[34] *Ibid.,* p. 33. My italics.

had been right after all; but that it was only because something real and objective and totally unexpected had actually happened at Easter that the disciples became changed men. I did not discuss the other possibility. My reason for this was because ·I find it incredible . . .[35]

By the time when he gave his Bampton Lectures in 1976, however, his views had undergone a fundamental change. He is still willing to assert, of course, that Paul 'certainly believed that the substance of the Gospel depended on the truth of the testimony that God did raise Jesus; for the raising of Jesus was his vindication by God'. Now, however, he not only questions how far the apostle identifies 'God's vindication of Jesus with an actual event in the physical world',[36] but asserts that it is 'very difficult indeed to determine' how far the 'appearance' to Paul himself

> was really different from the experiences of other believers: that is to say, how far it implied a personal presence of a risen Jesus, or how far it might be interpreted as a divine revelation, a reaching out of God's Spirit to the human spirit, that Paul apprehended in terms of Jesus, somewhat in the way in which the revelation to Bernadette was apprehended in terms of Mary.[37]

Inevitably, then one asks oneself what has happened to cause such a radical change of view; and the answer is not far to seek. It is not that the historical evidence, or the interpretation to which it most naturally points, has itself changed, but that the theological implications of coming to believe in 'Spirit Christology' have been worked out to their logical conclusion.

The result is an almost complete *volte face*, so that Lampe now writes

[35] *Ibid.*, p. 30.
[36] *Op. cit.*, pp. 146f.
[37] *Ibid.*, p. 148.

Neither these stories nor those of the empty tomb can help us much in trying to answer the question whether the 'appearances' actually generated the conviction that Jesus had been vindicated and exalted, or whether they were visual and aural experiences resulting from, and expressive of, that belief. . . . According to all the early traditions, the appearances in fact occurred only to those who were already disciples of Jesus (James being the one person in Paul's list of whose attitude to Jesus before his 'Easter experience' we know practically nothing), or, in Paul's case, already knew enough about him and about the beliefs of his followers to react with violent hostility. All these people were likely to 'see' the risen Jesus because they either believed that he would be vindicated by God or feared that he had been.[38]

But this is precisely the view that, in 1966, he had dismissed as 'incredible'. He concludes, moreover, that

However this may be, it does not seem that the present-day Christian's experience of the living Christ, which appears to be identical with experience of God as the Spirit that was in Jesus, is dependent upon the reliability of the traditions about the resurrection appearances or the empty tomb. Belief in Christ as a contemporary presence does not rest upon an assurance that the resurrection of Jesus actually happened as an event in history.[39]

But I am myself convinced that Lampe's former, and diametrically opposite, view was much more convincing. How can one speak meaningfully about 'the living Christ' or about his 'contemporary presence' when one is not in fact referring to Christ himself but to the Spirit who was in the 'Man of Nazareth' nearly two thousand years ago? It is true,

[38] *Ibid.*, pp. 149f.
[39] *Ibid.*, p. 150.

of course, that it is through the Holy Spirit that the risen, exalted Lord is made known to us today, as he himself promised. But surely Moule is right when he affirms that Paul conceives of the living Christ 'as more than individual, while still knowing him vividly and distinctly as fully personal';[40] that the other New Testament writers 'all identify the risen Lord as Jesus of Nazareth', although they 'clearly see him as more than an exalted and glorified human being';[41] and that nowhere in the New Testament

> is there any suggestion that Christian experience meant no more than that it was the teaching and example of a figure of the past which now enabled Christians to approach God with a new understanding and confidence, or that it was merely because of what Jesus had done and been in the past that they found the Spirit of God lifting them up to new capacities and powers. On the contrary, they believed that it was because the same Jesus was alive and was in some way in touch with them there and then that the new relationship and the new freedom were made possible... The transcendent, divine person of present experience was continuous and identical with the historical figure of the past.[42]

It is 'surprising', in Lampe's view, that the early Church 'made relatively little use' of the concept of Spirit-possession 'in trying to give a rational account of the relation of Jesus to God'.[43] Instead,

> the most remarkable fact about the historical Jesus is demonstrably true: that the earliest Christian documents show that within an astonishingly short time after his death Jesus of Nazareth was being interpreted by Jewish monotheists as well as Gentile converts as a pre-existent divine being, Son of God, not

---

[40] *The Origin of Christology*, p. 95.
[41] *Ibid.*, p. 98.
[42] *Ibid.*, pp. 98f.
[43] *Christ, Faith and History*, p. 118.

simply in the sense of Ps. 2:7 as God's agent for the establishment of his Kingdom but in a sense approaching that of 'God the Son' of later orthodoxy, to whom prayer is addressed and whom believers expect to come from heaven in divine glory (cf. 1 Th. 3:11, 1:10).[44]

Yet Spirit-possession, in Lampe's opinion, would have been a much more appropriate model.

God's Spirit is his own active presence: God himself reaching out to his creation . . . The Spirit may possess a man and in some measure unite his personality to God. Yet this is without any diminution of his humanity: rather, it means the raising of his humanity to its full potentiality, the completion of the human creation by the re-creating influence of the creator-Spirit. Through Spirit-possession a man may be divinely motivated and act divinely – he may be at one with God – and become at the same time, and because of this, fully and completely human.[45]

So a Spirit Christology would have provided 'a good foundation for the Nicene assertion that the deity we recognise in Christ is the deity of God in his own being, and nothing less', on the one hand, and for 'a full appreciation of the truth that Christ is the "proper man",' on the other.[45] It is the perfection of Christ's humanity which is so 'difficult to reconcile with the Alexandrian formulation of the Logos/Son Christology', he affirms, for

However strongly this Christology may maintain that the human nature assumed by the Logos/Son was complete manhood ('flesh ensouled with a rational soul'), it cannot easily find room for the balancing

[44] *The Expository Times*, 'The Essence of Christianity', in Feb., 1976, p. 133.
[45] *Christ, Faith and History*, p. 117.
[46] *Ibid.*, p. 118.

Antiochene and Chalcedonian insistence that Christ is of one essence with ourselves in respect of his humanity ... The classical affirmation that the Word became man, but not a man, indicates that once Christian thought had *identified* the person of Jesus with the Logos/Son ... it was set on a course which was bound to lead to a reductionist doctrine of Christ's manhood. ... Christology could then avoid this conclusion only by developing the idea of *kenōsis* to the point where, in order to become incarnate as true man, 'made like these brothers of his in every way' (Heb. 2:17), the divine Person has virtually divested himself of deity.

We shall grapple with the problems inherent in the classical Christology in my next chapter. What concerns us now is Lampe's preference for 'an interpretation of the person of Christ in terms of the "possession" of a man by God', which, he insists, would involve 'no diminution of either deity or humanity'.[47]

But this is clearly an equivocal statement. Lampe's Spirit Christology certainly involves no diminution in the humanity of Jesus, or in the deity of the divine Spirit who 'possessed' him; but it inevitably leads to a diminution – and, I think, a basic denial – of the deity of Jesus himself. In his essay on 'The Holy Spirit and the person of Christ' he himself emphasises that 'a primary question which confronts the advocates of such a Christology is whether the assertion that in Jesus God encounters us claims as much as the classical affirmation that Jesus *is* God'. 'Spirit Christology cannot affirm that Jesus *is* "substantively" God', he says, but

It does not follow that Jesus is only 'adjectivally' God, that is to say, God-*like* or divine in the sense of being a man who possessed to an excellent degree the qualities we attribute to God. An interpretation of the union of Jesus with God in terms of his total possession by

[47] *Ibid.*, pp. 119f.

God's Spirit makes it possible, rather, to acknowledge him to be God 'adverbially'. By the mutual interaction of the Spirit's influence and the free response of the human spirit such a unity of will and operation was established that in all his actions the human Jesus acted divinely.[48]

In his Bampton Lectures, moreover, he expresses what is essentially the same thought when he declares:

> I believe in the Divinity of our Lord and Saviour Jesus Christ, in the sense that the one God, the Creator and Saviour Spirit, revealed himself and acted decisively for us in Jesus. I believe in the Divinity of the Holy Ghost, in the sense that the same one God, the Creator and Saviour Spirit, is here and now not far from every one of us; for in him we live and move, in him we have our being, in us, if we consent to know and trust him, he will create the Christlike harvest: love, joy, peace, patience, kindness, goodness, fidelity, gentleness, and self-control.[49]

But, for all the warmth of Lampe's faith in this 'one God, the Creator and Saviour Spirit', and the Christlikeness of his character, it seems to me inescapable that this thesis is basically unitarian in nature.[50]

It is not altogether surprising, therefore, that in *God as Spirit* Lampe allows himself to make a number of highly questionable assertions. 'It is not possible for us, as it was for the ancients, to speak of Christ's presence having been withdrawn from earth to heaven, and of ourselves waiting for Christ to come again from heaven in glory,' he observes.[51] But I myself find it perfectly possible to speak in this way – provided, of course, the withdrawal of Christ's presence is understood in terms of his physical or visible presence. Again, he gets very close to giving a caricature of

---

48 *Christ, Faith and History*, pp. 123f.   50 Cf. *ibid.*, pp. 226ff.
49 *God as Spirit*, p. 228.   51 *Ibid.*, p. 6. Cf. also pp. 170f.

the classical doctrine of the atonement, whether in the form of a victory over the power of sin and Satan, or of a propitiation or expiation for the sins which inevitably separate us from a holy God.[52] It is quite inadequate to argue that 'the abandonment of the notion of an historical Fall removes the necessity to see redemption as the retrieving of a catastrophic reverse in the evolution of mankind'[53]; for it seems to me far more realistic, as well as biblical, to believe in a 'Fall', the grievous effects of which are everywhere apparent, than to try to convince oneself, against a weight of evidence, that man is steadily climbing towards perfection. And it is false to the biblical revelation, as I understand it, to deny that we have been redeemed from the just judgment of God by 'an objectively efficacious act';[54] although it is essential to remember that the propitiation which averts God's holy 'wrath' is itself the supreme demonstration of his love. It is not so much that the propitiation has issued in grace, as that grace prompted and provided the propitiation. To me the very quintessence of the Gospel is enshrined in the glorious affirmation: 'Herein is love, not that we loved God, but that he loved us, and sent his Son to be the propitiation for our sins'.[55] But this is, self-evidently, an impossible doctrine unless one believes that there was an essential identity between the God who 'sent' and the Son who 'came'. Here the model of the Spirit of God acting in and through one who was himself a 'mere' man is manifestly inadequate; and Athanasius was surely right when he insisted that 'the Saviour must be no less than God'; that 'Christ's saving work was unique, accomplished once for all, because it was carried out by a unique person'; and that 'this person is the one, eternal person of God the Son'[56] – 'made lower than the angels . . . so that by the grace of God he might taste death for every one.'[57]

---

[52] *Ibid.,* pp. 14-16, 102 etc.
[53] *Ibid.,* p. 34. Cf. pp. 18f.
[54] *Ibid.,* p. 97. Cf. pp. 14, 16 etc.
[55] 1 John 4:10.
[56] *Christ, Faith and History,* p. 120.
[57] Heb. 2:9.

Lampe, moreover, does not hesitate to assert that

> The Spirit of God who addresses us through the
> character of Christ . . . may move us to reject certain
> elements in the tradition of the words and deeds of
> Jesus as being incompatible with the general purport
> and implications of the divine revelation in Christ.
> Such elements sometimes belong to what source-
> criticism may fairly confidently assign to non-
> dominical strands in the tradition, but sometimes they
> can plausibly be attributed to Jesus himself. In the
> latter case the Spirit of Christ may be leading us
> beyond the historical Jesus, though into a fuller un-
> derstanding of the divine revelation which had the
> historical Jesus at its centre.[58]

Predictably enough, the examples Lampe gives of the
latter are the exchanges between Jesus and 'the Jews' in the
Fourth Gospel and the passages about eternal punishment
in the Synoptic Gospels. But among the many questions to
which this whole subject gives rise, the query posed by
Nineham in his Epilogue to *The Myth of God Incarnate* is
particularly pertinent. When applied specifically to Lampe
this can be expressed by asking how he can really be sure
that 'God indwelt and motivated the human spirit of Jesus in
such a way that in him, uniquely, the relationship for which
man is intended by his Creator was fully realised';[59] that 'we
can speak of the life of Jesus as God's self-revelation, no
longer dimmed and distorted, as in other men, by the
opaqueness of sin in the mirror which reflects and com-
municates it';[60] that the 'interaction of divine Spirit with
human spirit presents itself to us, and takes effect in us, in
terms of the character, actions and words of Jesus';[61] that in
'the portrayal in the Gospels of his way of life, focussed in his

---

[58] *God as Spirit*, pp. 109f.
[59] *Ibid.*, p. 11.
[60] *Ibid.*, p. 24.
[61] *Ibid.*, pp. 24f.

death as the key to the understanding of his life, there is to be found the supreme revelation of the relationship between God and man ... the great transforming and redemptive disclosure of God's judgment, compassion and love'[62]; and much else in the same vein. We have already seen how Lampe's Spirit Christology has caused him radically to revise his convictions about the resurrection; and it is difficult to see why this same process should not be carried considerably further. If there are adequate grounds for believing that Jesus, while truly man, was also truly God – a subject to which we shall return in my next chapter – then all this, and much more, can be predicated of him. But if he was no more than a man possessed or indwelt by the divine Spirit, then what warrant have we, on a highly critical view of all the historical evidence, for asserting that he was, in fact, 'uniquely' or 'fully' Spirit-possessed, that this was his constant experience, and that we can, with confidence and integrity, make the claims for him that Lampe does not hesitate to make? In other words, is this truncated Christology viable, on strictly critical grounds, today? Personally, I do not think it is; and I am confirmed in my belief by an article on 'Alternative Versions of Christian Faith' by Dr. Margaret Thrall.[63]

Even if it were *viable,* however, the question remains whether such a Christology is *adequate.* Frankly, I do not myself believe that it is. We have already seen that it does not provide a basis for *any* objective view of the atonement, but only for an 'exemplarist' doctrine of some sort. It cannot even be said that the fact that 'Christ died for us while we were yet sinners' constitutes, on this basis, 'God's own proof of his love towards us';[64] for how can the death of a man in whom God was only 'adverbially' present provide any convincing evidence for God's own love? Nor, in my view, is it in any way adequate as an affirmation of authentic Christian experience. It is true that Lampe, in his essay in

[62] *Christian Believing,* p. 111.
[63] *The Expository Times,* Jan. 1977 (LXXXVIII. No. 4).
[64] Rom. 5:8 NEB. And what basic purpose would it serve?

1972, asserted that 'a Christology of inspiration and possession states no less clearly than a Christology of substance
that in the person of Jesus Christ God has taken human
nature and from the moment of birth or before has made it
his own'; but he says that the 'appropriate analogy for this
union of man with God is, as has often been pointed out,
that of grace, summed up in the Pauline "not I, indeed, but
the grace of God working with me" (1 Cor. 15:10).'[65] So in
his essay in 1972 Lampe proceeded to ponder the question
'why there has been only one Incarnation, and why it should
be assumed that there will never be another?'[66] To this the
answers he suggested were, I think, far from convincing, and
he has not repeated them; for in terms of Spirit Christology
the question seems to me to be unanswerable.

But Paul and John, and the other New Testament writers,
would certainly not have been satisfied with any such
Christology. Instead, as Lampe himself insists in *God as
Spirit,* 'they wished to affirm the personal pre-existence of
Jesus Christ as Son of God, the continuing personal "post-
existence" of Jesus Christ, resurrected and ascended and
also experienced by present believers, and the future return
of the ascended Christ in glory.'[67] This is the faith that the
Christian Church has always professed, and I agree with Dr.
Thrall that the views of many contemporary theologians

> confront the Church with the necessity of making a
> choice. It must either declare itself obsolete, and
> recognise that its life and beliefs are no more than an
> interesting chapter in the history of religions, or else it
> must make a much more strenuous and convincing
> attempt to formulate the traditional faith of the creeds
> in terms which are acceptable with intellectual integrity
> today.[68]

[65] Cf. pp. 113 and 122 above.
[66] *Christ, Faith and History,* p. 126.
[67] p. 119.
[68] *Op. cit.,* p. 16.

6
The Incarnation and Personal Faith Today

MY FIRST LECTURE IN THIS SERIES ON 'THE MYSTERY OF the Incarnation' took the form of a general introduction to the subject and an attempt to etch in the background to what I have termed 'The Contemporary Debate'. Starting from the basic Christian confession, 'Jesus is Lord', we looked first at some of the titles applied to Jesus in the Gospels – Son of Man, Christ, Son of God, Lord – and the exceedingly strong evidence there is for the vivid consciousness he had of a unique filial relationship with his heavenly Father, unclouded by any sense of personal sin; for the innate authority which characterised his words and actions; and for his constant response to the divine imperative which called him, ever more clearly, to 'give his life a ransom for many'. We saw, too, how his disciples, completely misunderstanding the nature of his mission, were thrown into despair, with all their hopes shattered, by his betrayal and execution. *But God raised him from the dead,* and thereby brought them back – wondering, and at first doubting their very senses – to a living hope and a triumphant joy. His resurrection and exaltation led them to see him in an entirely new light; and this was why they now felt compelled to call him 'Lord' and began to associate him with God himself in prayer and worship.

How, then, did they now view his earthly life, during which they must, beyond doubt, have regarded him as a man among men; and how did they explain his new status? One suggestion, which (as we have seen) assumes quite a prominent place in the contemporary debate, can be summed up in the term Adoptionism – that is, that God at some stage 'adopted' him as his Son, and exalted him to a place of lordship and power;

and we saw that this is regarded by many writers today as the earliest Christology. It is clear, however, that the Church of the middle of the first century did not only believe in the exaltation of 'the man, Christ Jesus', but also in his pre-existence, for we find references to this from a very early date – and without any explanation or comment – in several of St. Paul's Epistles. It would have been natural enough, of course, to reason that a life which the early Church believed to be 'eternal' in the sense that it would have no end must equally be eternal in the sense of having no beginning; but I for one have no doubt that the concept can also be traced back to the way in which Jesus himself had sometimes spoken.

Several contemporary writers, however, insist that this concept of 'pre-existence' must be interpreted exclusively in terms of God's fore-knowledge, purpose and plan that in the fullness of time a man would be born in whom he could and would uniquely reveal himself. Anything more than that, they maintain, would inevitably compromise the humanity of Jesus and lead to some form of 'psychological Docetism' – or a belief that Jesus was not really human (and certainly not 'a particular man'), but God in human guise.

So, in my second lecture, I attempted to trace, in outline, the history of christological thought down the centuries. Starting with the extremes of Gnostic Docetism, which did not regard Jesus as a real man at all, on the one hand, and those Jewish Ebionites who denied that he was other than a purely human Messiah, on the other, we touched on the Arian, Apollinarian and Nestorian heresies, discussed the Nicene Creed and the Definition of Chalcedon, and noted the continuing differences between the Alexandrian and Antiochene schools of thought, the controversy between Monophysites and Dyophysites, and the divisions of opinion between Lutheran and Reformed theologians and even within the Lutheran communion. In part these controversies were based on purely philosophical distinctions; and the protracted disputes about whether the human nature of Christ must be predicated of a human *hypostasis* or entity, or might be predicated of a divine *hypostasis,* do not, *per se,* seem very meaningful today. Broadly speaking, however, it may be said that the Antiochenes held firmly to the view that our Lord was truly man as well as God, but at the expense of depicting him, at times, as a completely split personality, acting first in the one capacity and then in the other; whereas the Alexandrians emphasised the unity of his person and his essential deity, but at the expense of minimising his true humanity. And the same basic problem has recurred, in somewhat different forms, all down the ages, for how could he be really God and really man – either alternately or at one and the same time? How could the divine Logos or Son of God – himself, by definition, transcendent, omnipotent and allegedly impassible – become incarnate in a baby or suffer as a man? How could he be omnipresent when lying in his mother's arms? How could he be omniscient, and yet have to learn like other boys? And how could he uphold the universe by his word of power as a sleeping baby – or even as boy or man?

It may have sufficed, at one time, to say that 'the impassible Logos suffered in the passible flesh' or 'usefully pretended not to know'; but such phrases seem little better than quibbles today. It may have been possible to agree on Creeds and Definitions which would serve to define the bounds of orthodoxy and exclude unacceptable deviations; but how can Christians of a later age come to any understanding of the Jesus who, we read, shared our nature, grew in wisdom and stature, was in all points tempted as we are, and learned obedience in the school of suffering – and yet, as the Church has always believed, was the Word made flesh, the image of the invisible God, the Lord through whom all things were created, and the Saviour who tasted death for every man? To talk of a 'person' in this age of psychology means to think of a real, living personality, with all that this has come to mean, not a philosophical abstraction. So how can the Christian confession that Jesus is Lord be meaningful and relevant for us in the twentieth century?

One of the major ways of attempting to solve the mystery of how the Son or Logos, sharing all the attributes of the

Godhead, could be incarnate in the man Jesus, has been through the doctrine of *kenōsis,* or self-emptying. This doctrine is based, in part, on the statement in Philippians 2:5-8 that, 'though he was in the form of God', Christ 'did not count equality with God a thing to be grasped, but emptied himself, taking the form of a slave, being born in the likeness of men. And being found in human form he humbled himself . . .' In part, however, it may be said to be quite independent of this much-quoted passage and to be inherent in the obvious fact that, when 'the Word became flesh', this must have entailed some limitation of the *manifest* glory of deity, at the very least. As such the concept of *kenōsis* was not unknown to the Fathers; but Pannenberg insists that 'Origen, Athanasius, Gregory of Nyssa, Cyril of Alexandria, Augustine and others who connected Phil. 2:7 to the coming of the Logos in the flesh meant by the term "self-emptying" the assumption of human nature, but not the complete or partial relinquishment of the divine nature or its attributes'.[1] We have already seen, moreover, how in the seventeenth and eighteenth centuries the theologians of Tübingen under the leadership of Johann Brenz believed that Jesus not only possessed the divine attributes of omnipotence, omniscience and omnipresence from the time of his birth, but actually on occasions used them in a way which was concealed from others, while Martin Chemnitz – who equally believed that Jesus retained all his divine attributes – thought in terms not of concealment *(krysis)* but a partial refusal to use them. Eventually, however, the doctrine of the theologians of Giessen, which involved a real renunciation *(kenōsis)* of their use during the state of Christ's 'humiliation', triumphed. Turner, indeed, asserts that this distinction between the 'two states' – the state of Christ's humiliation and the state of his exaltation – represents the most distinctive contribution of the Reformation to Christology. But while the Lutherans regarded this *kenōsis* as representing a continual concealment of the divine glory, or renunciation of the use of divine

Pannenberg, *op. cit.,* p. 308 – citing F. Loofs.

attributes, by the incarnate Lord (so that 'the God-man of this Christology' – to quote Pannenberg – remained a sort of fabulous being, more like a mythical redeemer than the historical reality of Jesus of Nazareth)[2], the theologians of the Reformed Churches thought in terms of some sort of initial *kenōsis* by the pre-incarnate Son at the time when he became incarnate.[3]

It was this last concept which was the starting point for the remarkable development of the 'Kenotic Theory' in the nineteenth and earlier twentieth centuries. Thus Thomasius, in Germany, taught that at the Incarnation the divine Son 'gave up the relative attributes of divinity, that is, those which characterise the *relation* of God to the world: omnipotence, omniscience, omnipresence', and 'retained only the *immanent* perfections proper to God independent of his relation to the world: holiness, power, truth, and love'. It was in this way, he believed, that we could understand the human life of Jesus without any abandonment of his divine essence or life.[4] In the Incarnation the Logos 'exchanged His divine consciousness for one that was human, or rather Divine-human; and thus became capable of forming the centre of a single personal Life'. In other words, he 'voluntarily contracted His life to the form and dimensions of human existence, submitting to the laws of human growth and preserving His absolute powers only in the measure in which they were essential to His redeeming work; and at the close of His earthly career He resumed once more the glory he had laid aside'.[5] This may be said to represent the classical form of the Kenotic Theory; but there are, of course, numerous variations. Gess, for example, went so far as to interpret the Incarnation as 'a transformation of the Logos into a human soul' – which Thomasius regarded as an 'abandonment of his divinity'.[6]

[2] Pannenberg, *op. cit.,* p. 309.
[3] Mackintosh, *op. cit.,* p. 243.
[4] Cf. Pannenberg, *op. cit.,* p. 310.
[5] Mackintosh, *op. cit.,* p. 266.
[6] Pannenberg, *op. cit.,* p. 7.

But the Kenotic Theory has been strongly criticised on a number of different grounds. First, it has been repeatedly emphasised that Phil. 2:5-11 should not be regarded as a theological exposition of any such doctrine, but rather as an ethical exhortation to Christian humility based on the example of the humility of Christ himself – and it is significant in this context that the phrase *heanton ekanōsen* in Phil. 2:7, literally translated 'emptied himself' in the RSV, is rendered 'made himself of no reputation' in the AV and 'made himself nothing' in the NEB. Secondly, the Kenotic *Theory,* as such, has been criticised as failing to give any explanation of how the divine Son or Logos continued to uphold the universe by his word of power (Heb. 1:3) during his incarnate life. As Temple put it: 'To say that the Infant Jesus was from His cradle exercising providential care over it all is certainly monstrous; but to deny this, and yet to say that the Creative Word was so self-emptied as to have no being except in the Infant Jesus, is to assert that for a certain period the history of the world was let loose from the control of the Creative Word'.[7] Again, the theory has been criticised as failing to do justice either to the deity of Jesus during the days of his flesh or to the humanity of the exalted Lord. In D. M. Baillie's words: 'Instead of giving us a doctrine of Incarnation in which Jesus Christ is both God and man, the Kenotic Theory appears to me to give us a story of a temporary theophany, in which He who formerly was God changed Himself temporarily into man, or exchanged His divinity for humanity.' If, moreover, the Incarnation itself is explained as *kenōsis,* this presumably came to an end with his exaltation. So, in the Kenotic Theory in its extreme form, 'He is God and Man, not simultaneously in a hypostatic union, but *successively* – first divine, then human, then God again.' But this 'seems to leave no room at all for the traditional catholic doctrine of the *permanence* of the manhood of Christ "who, being the eternal Son of God, became man, and so was, and *continueth to be,* God and

---

[7] *Christus Veritas,* pp. 142f.

man in two distinct natures, and one person, *for ever*"'.[8]

We must return to this subject shortly. But at this point I must, I think, begin to attempt to outline the conclusions to which I have myself come, after quite a lot of mental wrestling. They will, of course, inevitably be inadequate, not only because of my own deficiencies as an amateur theologian, but also because no finite mind can hope to plumb the unrevealed secrets of the Godhead or the mystery of the Incarnation. So I will content myself with summarising my conclusions in the form of two basic principles and a number of tentative propositions.

The first principle that I regard as fundamental is that we must do our utmost to grapple with the biblical evidence as a whole and see where this leads us, rather than put an exclusive – and perhaps exaggerated – emphasis on certain parts of that evidence and explain away, or ignore, anything which may seem to point in a different direction. It is obvious that different New Testament writers had their own distinctive insights and modes of expression; that the way in which any member of the early Church wrote, or is reported to have spoken, must have been greatly influenced by the particular context in which he wrote or the audience he was addressing; and that they were all struggling to clothe in words an experience and a mystery they had only very partially apprehended. But I am myself convinced that Professor Moule is right when he suggests that 'development' is a more appropriate analogy than 'evolution' for the way in which 'descriptions and understandings of Jesus' emerged; for if evolution 'means the genesis of successive new species by mutation and natural selection', development, by contrast, 'will mean something more like the growth, from immaturity to maturity, of a single specimen from within itself'. So he challenges 'the tendency to explain the change from (say) invoking Jesus as a revered Master to the acclamation of him as a divine Lord by the theory that,

---

[8] Cf. D. M. Baillie, *op. cit.,* pp. 96f., with the final quotation taken from the *Westminster Shorter Catechism* (his italics).

when the Christian movement spread beyond Palestinian soil, it began to come under the influence of non-Semitic Saviour-cults'; or, indeed, to attempt to explain the change by appeal to the effect of 'lapse of time, which may itself lead to the intensification of terms of adoration'. Instead, he believes the evidence suggests that 'all the various estimates of Jesus reflected in the New Testament' are, in essence, 'only attempts to describe what was there from the beginning. They are not successive additions of something new, but only the drawing out and articulating of what is there'. Moreover, 'when one assumes that the changes are, in the main, changes only in perception', it becomes clear that 'it may not be possible, *a priori,* to arrange such changes in any firm chronological order. In evolution, the more complex species generally belong to a later stage than the more simple; but in development, there is nothing to prevent a profoundly perceptive estimate occurring at an early stage . . .' This is not, of course, to suggest that Moule wants 'to eliminate the chronological factor altogether'. What he does assert unequivocally is that the evidence, as he sees it, 'suggests that Jesus was, *from the beginning,* such a one as appropriately to be described in the ways in which, sooner or later, he did come to be described in the New Testament period – for instance as "Lord" and even, in some sense, as "God".'[9]

If, then, we try to take the biblical evidence as a whole more seriously than many participants in the contemporary debate, we shall certainly insist that the Word was, in very fact, 'made flesh', and that Jesus was truly man. But we shall not regard his 'total solidarity with all men', in the sense that he was, in himself (or ontologically), *only* human, 'without remainder', as the fundamental criterion by reference to which everything which the New Testament tells us about his earthly life, his pre-existence and his present exaltation must be measured, interpreted or even discarded. Instead, we must do all we possibly can to find a solution to the very

[9] *The Origin of Christology,* pp. 1-4.

real problems inherent in Christology that takes due account of *all* the available evidence. For this virtually our only primary authority is the New Testament – supported, of course, by Christian experience down the centuries. But I see no reason to suppose that the testimony of the New Testament on this subject is either false or misleading. On the contrary, if God did in fact act, uniquely and decisively, in Jesus for the world's salvation – and for this I find the evidence wholly convincing – then it seems to me inherently unlikely that he would have left the basic facts and implications of that action without any reliable records and trustworthy teaching about their meaning.

My second fundamental principle is that no understanding of the mystery of the Incarnation can be true to the biblical revelation unless it also explains the meaning and significance of the Atonement. Any Christology which concentrates on Emmanuel, God with us, at the expense of Jesus, God the Saviour, must surely be defective; for soteriology and Christology are inextricably bound together. This has, of course, often been emphasised – notably, in recent years, by H. E. W. Turner. But it is significant, I think, that all those who insist on a Christology which regards Christ as exclusively human, even if the locus or agent of a uniquely divine revelatory event, take a subjective rather than objective view of the Atonement – or, to be more precise, a view which concentrates on the subjective effect on man of what they would certainly accept as an objective event. Those of us, on the other hand, who regard the Atonement as of fundamental importance, not only because of the subjective change it can, should, and does effect in man and his attitude to God, but also because it provides the essential basis on which, alone, a holy God can and does proffer a full and free forgiveness to the repentant sinner – free to him because the God who proffers it has redeemed him at so great a cost – must necessarily, I believe, find this Christology inadequate.

If, for example, we accept that the biblical doctrine of the Atonement clearly includes, among its many different

meanings and facets, the fact that Christ died not only on
our behalf but in our place, or in any sense as a 'sacrifice for
sin', then it would be monstrous to believe that 'God was
reconciling the world to himself' in (or by) an entirely
innocent and purely human being whom he 'made sin for us',
and who thus 'bore our sins in his body on the tree.' The idea
would be utterly abhorrent. But that there *is* such an element
in the Atonement is expressed with his usual trenchancy by
Barth in his commentary on the last few verses in 2 Corinthians 5, where he writes about what he terms an *'exchange'*. 'This', he says, 'is what is expressly stated in the
verse (21) with which the passage closes. On the one side, the
exchange: 'He hath made him to be sin for us (in our place
and for our sake), who knew no sin . . . And on the other
side, the exchange: He does it, He takes our place in Christ,
that we (again in the simplest possible form) might be made
the righteousness of God (δικαιοσύνη θεοῦ) in Him'. Later,
he continues: 'At this point we can and must make the
decisive statement: What took place is that the Son of God
fulfilled the righteous judgment on us men by Himself
taking our place as man and in our place undergoing the
judgment under which we had passed.' Elsewhere,
moreover, he asserts that 'Jesus Christ for us signifies His
activity as our Representative and Substitute . . . If someone
gives his life a λυτρον αντι πολλῶν (Mk. 10:45) then he
necessarily acts in the place and as the representative of the
πολλοί, paying on their account but without their co-
operation what they cannot pay for themselves.'[10] Similarly,
Pannenberg writes: 'Paul stressed that Jesus was without sin
precisely where he emphasised that Jesus was judged, cursed
(Galatians 3:13), treated as a sinner by God in our stead.
Only because Jesus was himself without sin can it be said
that what he suffered was not the consequence of his own

---

[10] *Church Dogmatics* IV (ed. G. W. Bromiley and T. F. Torrance, T. and T.
Clark, Edinburgh, 1960), Pt. I, pp. 75 and 222f. Cf. Richard Hooker (*Works,* Vol.
ii, p. 606) 'We care for no knowledge in the world but this, that man hath sinned and
God hath suffered; that God hath made Himself the sin of men, and that men are
made the righteousness of God.'

guilt, but that he took his suffering upon himself for our sake.'[11] This concept of God's 'curse' must, indeed, as Professor F. F. Bruce has persuasively argued, have been one of the earliest elements in Paul's thought. Before the experience on the Damascus road the statement in Deut. 21:23 that 'a hanged man is accursed by God' had, no doubt, sufficed to dismiss as impossible any suggestion of a crucified Messiah. But the resurrection had proved that the crucified Jesus was far from 'accursed' in himself. So 'sooner rather than later Paul must have reached the conclusion . . . that Jesus submitted to the death of the cross in order to take upon himself the curse which the law pronounced on all who failed to keep it completely (Deut. 27:26)'.[12]

The significance of this for Christology seems to me inescapable. No one who was in himself human *'and no more'* could bear the curse and judgment on our sins or be a 'sacrifice for sin' (for those who favour this translation of 2 Cor. 5:21 and Rom. 8:3); and the 'Son' whom the Father, in his infinite love, sent to be the propitiation or expiation for those sins must have been, in some basic sense (that is, ontologically, rather than functionally), one with the God who was, in him, 'reconciling the world to himself'.

In the light of these two basic principles, it seems to me that we can make the following propositions.

1. Before the Resurrection, the disciples clearly accepted the real manhood of Jesus as axiomatic: indeed, in the Synoptic Gospels, as has often been remarked, this is 'assumed rather than asserted', while in John's Gospel we find the positive assertion that the Word 'became flesh', together with repeated references to his manhood. His disciples – and many of those who heard his teaching and saw his works of love and power – realised that he was no ordinary man; but certainly did not yet identify him with God – or, still less, a sort of demi-god. There was nothing extraordinary, so far as we know, about his gestation and

---

[11] *Op. cit.,* p. 355.
[12] *The Epistle to the Romans* (Tyndale Press, London, 1963), pp. 36f.

birth; and although I fully believe in his virginal conception, this (as we have seen) was clearly not part of the basic apostolic *kerygma*. Both Jesus and his apostles called men to faith in him on the basis of his life, death and, supremely, his resurrection, not stories or assertions about his nativity.

He seems in most ways, moreover, outwardly to have been a perfectly normal boy. As John Robinson vividly expresses it, there is something unnatural about the statement in a well-known Christmas hymn 'The little Lord Jesus no crying he makes'; and the line from another Christmas hymn 'Tears and smiles like us he knew' seems to strike a much more authentic note. But I said 'in most ways' deliberately, since the evidence both for his sinlessness and for his unique filial consciousness is exceedingly strong; so his sinlessness must have extended right back to his boyhood; and his filial consciousness, while it must have dawned gradually, seems to have started at a very early age. But throughout his whole earthly life the Jesus of the Gospels strikes us as an essentially integrated personality, who was accepted everywhere as genuinely human and was the welcome guest of 'tax collectors and sinners'. He grew in body, mind and understanding as other boys grow; he was tempted as we are; he learnt obedience in the school of suffering; and, while he often spoke to his heavenly Father in profound tranquillity and confident assurance, he could and did pray to him 'with loud cries and tears', for in Gethsemane 'anguish and dismay came over him, and he said "My heart is ready to break with grief".' It is clear moreover, that he not only had a human body and 'rational soul' but a human will which shrank from the agony he knew was to be his, although this will was always kept subject to that of his Father.

But we must also make room in our assessment for the more than ordinary knowledge of men's hearts and circumstances which he sometimes showed and the works of love and power which he performed. The former could conceivably be explained in terms of extra-sensory perception, and his 'mighty works' can be attributed, like those of the prophets and apostles, to divine power. But alongside these we must take due account of that innate authority with which he spoke and acted; those claims (explicitly in his words and implicitly in his deeds) which the Jews regarded as blasphemous; and the way in which he moved others to shame and repentance yet showed no consciousness whatever of personal unworthiness or even the experience of forgiven sins.

2.   But the watershed, from the point of view of his disciples, was clearly the resurrection. Only after that do we find him regarded as 'Lord' in the full sense of that word, referred to and addressed as the 'Lord Jesus' and instinctively accorded a divine status. But we have already seen that the resurrection could not *of itself* have proved that he was 'Son of God' (Rom. 1:3): it was because of the life he had lived and the claims he had made that the apostolic Church insisted that the fact that God had 'raised him from the dead' must be regarded as the divine endorsement both of his Sonship and of the efficacy of his atoning death. Nor was his resurrection a mere resuscitation to terrestial life, but the beginning of a new life of exaltation in which his spiritual presence was made real to his disciples by the promised Holy Spirit.

It was in the light of his exaltation, I believe, that they remembered words he had spoken during his earthly life which they had been totally unable to understand at the time. I fully agree with Moule that their wide-spread belief, at a very early date, in his pre-existence *could* have been based solely on a logical inference from their experience of the exalted Jesus 'in a dimension transcending the human and the temporal' – a 'divine dimension such that he must always and eternally have existed in it.' The Jesus they had known on earth had retained 'his *personal identity*' after his resurrection and ascension; so must not that personal identity have also existed before his birth at Bethlehem? Where I differ from Moule is when he states that it is difficult 'to conceive of a genuinely human person being conscious of his own pre-existence'. In general terms this is undoubtedly true; but if Jesus, while 'genuinely human', was also God expressing himself in truly human terms (as Moule believes), and if he not only had a vivid consciousness of his relationship to his Father but a complete dependence on the Father's power and teaching, might not some intimation of his pre-incarnate life have been revealed to him? For myself, I am content to believe that John 17:5 represents a memory of 'Jesus' *ipsissima vox*.[13]

It was consequent on his exaltation, too, that an embryonic belief in the Trinity must have begun to emerge. The confession 'Jesus is Lord', with all that the title *kyrios* implies, proves that at a very early date the exalted Saviour was somehow identified with God. This may have come naturally enough to Gentile converts; but in the case of Paul the Pharisee and his like, to whom the unity of the Godhead was absolutely fundamental, it is deeply significant. The Johannine reference to the fact that 'the Word was with God, and the Word was God' (pointing, as it does, to a differentiation existing within a basic identity) – coupled with, or preceded by, the allusions in St. Paul's letters and in Hebrews to the One who is the 'image of the invisible God', the 'Son of his love', through whom 'all things were made' and in whom 'all things subsist' – mark the beginning of a theology which was later expanded as a result of the experienced presence of the promised Holy Spirit. The doctrine of the Trinity as such falls outside the scope of these lectures; but I must remark in passing that – while the view that the distinction between Father, Son and (subsequently) Holy Spirit should be understood solely in terms of different 'modes' in which God acted in creation, revelation and redemption[14] (rather than in terms of 'subsisting relations' or 'centres of consciousness' within the unity of the Godhead) does not seem to me to take adequate account, *inter alia*, of the mutual and eternal love of the Father and

---

[13] For Moule's views on these points, cf. (inter alia) *The Origin of Christology*, pp. 138f.

[14] To lump together 'Modalism', the concept of the 'Economic Trinity' and other similar concepts.

the Son – the basic truth of the divine Unity should restrain us from ever thinking of the 'Persons' of the Trinity as in any sense separate individuals (which would, of course, amount to Tri-theism). And this, in turn, should suffice to indicate that while it was, indeed, in the Word or Son that 'God was manifest in the flesh', this does not mean that 'the man, Christ Jesus' was pre-existent as such,[15] or that the eternal Word was not still performing his cosmic functions during the years when he was incarnate in Jesus. But we shall have to return to this point a little later.

3. What I have already said will, I think, explain why I do not believe that any inspirational, rather than incarnational – or functional, rather than ontological – Christology will meet our need. It is true that some of the scholars I have quoted go as far as they possibly can, on their premises, in giving a unique place to Jesus, and that they believe that he was, indeed, the 'human face of God' and the 'exegesis of the Father'; but they insist that that face was in itself purely human and no more. And on this basis I cannot see any justification whatever for according worship even to the exalted Christ, or for ever addressing him in prayer. Few Christians, I think, would be content to explain their 'encounter' with the risen Christ in worship and prayer as being 'encountered by God, the Spirit who was in Jesus, meeting them with the identical judgment, mercy, forgiveness and love which were at work with Jesus'[16] – for this would be to eliminate the mediation, priesthood and intercession of the One they believe to be still man as well as God.[17] I cannot believe that a 'Spirit' or merely 'inspirational' Christology does justice to such a basic statement as 'for you know the grace of our Lord Jesus Christ, that though he was rich, yet for your sakes he became poor,

---

[15] Cf. E. L. Mascall, *Theology and the Gospel of Christ* (SPCK, London 1977), pp. 180f.

[16] Cf. 'The Holy Spirit and the person of Christ' by G. W. F. Lampe, in *Christ, Faith and History*, p. 130.

[17] Lampe has discussed this subject much more fully in *God as Spirit* (The Bampton Lectures for 1976, Clarendon Press, Oxford, 1977), pp. 164ff.

so that by his poverty you might become rich (2 Cor. 8:9), or to the absolute uniqueness of the One who was not only 'separate from sinners' (Heb. 7:26) but in whom, and for whom, 'all things were created, in heaven and on earth' (Col. 1:16). Nor does it seem in any way adequate for the One almost certainly described as 'the only God, who is in the bosom of the Father', in John 1:18; to whom the author of the letter to the Hebrews probably attributes – specifically as Son – the title of 'God' (Heb. 1:8 and 9); whom St. Paul almost certainly calls 'God' in Romans 9:5;[18] and who is probably referred to as our 'God and Saviour' in Titus 2:3 and 2 Peter 1:11.[19]

4.   How, then, can we reconcile this essential deity with full human experience? This is the age-old problem. As we have seen, one way of expressing the testimony of the New Testament to both the true humanity and true deity of Jesus was the doctrine of the 'two natures'. And if, as I certainly believe, Christ was, and is, *vere deus, vere homo,* there is an essential – and virtually unquestionable – truth in saying that he must have had two natures. In Galot's words (as translated by Mascall): 'We cannot appreciate the character of the enterprise unless we recognise the divine transcendence of the person and the wholeness of the human condition in which it is involved; and this is what is expressed by the affirmation of the duality of the natures in Christ.'[20] But this doctrine in its developed form is almost inextricably bound up with the philosophical concept that 'nature' is a 'secondary substance' which must always be predicated of a *hypostasis* (or entity) as a 'primary sub-

---

[18] Cf. Metzger, *Christ and Spirit in the New Testament* (C.U.P. 1973), pp. 95-112.

[19] All the New Testament passages in which Jesus is probably, or possibly, referred to as 'God' are discussed in some detail in Arthur W. Wainwright, *The Trinity in the New Testament* (SPCK, London, 1975), pp. 53ff. Cf. also O. Cullman, *The Theology of the New Testament* (SCM Press, London, 1957), pp. 307ff.

[20] *Vers une nouvelle christologie* (Gembloux, Duculot; and Paris, Lethielleux, 1971), p. 48 –quoted in Mascall, *Theology and the Gospel of Christ* (SPCK, London, 1977), p. 174.

stance', and the consequent disputes between those whose understanding of the doctrine force them to depict Jesus as almost a split personality and those who regard him as so basically divine that his true humanity, while always asserted, becomes distinctly questionable.

The classical way in which this has been expressed has been by the affirmation that the eternal Son took to himself 'impersonal human nature'; that he became 'man' without becoming 'a particular man'. This means that his human nature was either devoid of a human *hypostasis* ('entity', 'subsistence' or 'primary substance') or found its identity in the Logos/Son: that is, to use the technical terms, that his human nature was *anhypostatos* or *enhypostatos*. Recently, however, it has repeatedly been asserted that any such concept 'totally fails to do justice to the reality and completeness of his humanity'. But we need to get behind the philosophical terms in which the classical doctrine is couched; for the concept of his 'impersonal' human nature should not be thought of as 'human nature in its generality', which would be a purely Platonic idea. The human nature of Jesus was certainly individual, and had distinctive qualities and characteristics. What the doctrine means is that his human nature had no personal subsistence distinct from that of the Logos; for if it had had a distinct 'personal' existence or entity of its own, then he would either have been two 'persons', in the modern understanding of personality, or he would have been no more than a man wholly 'possessed' or 'inspired' by God, as many affirm today. But the concept of his 'impersonal' human nature need not be so understood as to detract in any way from his genuine humanity: for the point at issue is simply that 'the human nature formed in and out of Mary did not for a moment exist by and for itself'. In other words, to speak of the 'impersonal' human nature of Christ in any context other than a purely theological and technical one would give a false impression which is very different from the picture of Jesus we get in the Gospels; but in the particular context of denying 'an independently conceived human nature' the term can be used 'without the connotation that some essential constituent of humanity is lacking in Christ'.[21]

But this does little or nothing to elucidate the mystery of how One who was truly God could also be truly man. It is precisely this which so many contemporary theologians dismiss as 'impossible', a 'contradiction in terms' or – at best – a 'myth'. But if the eternal Logos/Son was really incarnate in the man Christ Jesus (which seems to me a much fairer way of expressing the essence of the Nicene Creed and the Definition of Chalcedon than the 'descent of a pre-existent divine person into the world'), this must necessarily have involved a very real 'humiliation' or limitation of some sort. As we have seen, this has very generally been expressed, in recent years, in some variation of the Kenotic Theory. But I have already mentioned some of the objections which have been raised to that theory as such – among them the fact that Philippians 2:7, from which it derives its name, is taken from a passage which should not be regarded as a theological exposition of the incarnation so much as an ethical exhortation to Christian humility. Of this Moule aptly remarks: 'Of course there is no denying that the "pattern" of Phil. 2:5-11 as a whole is the pattern of descent followed by ascent, humiliation followed by exaltation.' But that, he believes, need not prevent one seeing, at the same time, a pattern 'by which height is *equated* with depth, humiliation is *identified* with exaltation'. And he continues:

> Anybody will recognise, for instance, that creative art involves an acceptance, and a positive use, of limitation. A craftsman in wood has to know all about the grain and the capacities of the wood he is working with, and, by accepting them and working with them, he exploits them to the full as a craftsman in wood-carving. So God the creator, when working in humanity, may be expected to express himself most fully, so far as the idiom of that medium goes, by accepting the

[21] Cf. G.P. Berkouwer, *The Person of Jesus* (Eerdmans, Grand Rapids, Michigan, 1954), pp. 306, 310f. and 321.

human range of capacity and exploiting the medium to the full. This is no more self-emptying than it is complete self-fulfilment in a given medium. . . . There is, it must be granted, an "emptying", a *kenōsis*, in respect of *scope,* even if this is in the interests of the "fulfilment", the *plērōsis,* of artistic *skill.* It is possible to recognise a change of "status", even if not of character. . . . But it would be a mistake if it were imagined that such language implied a deliberate renunciation of possibilities, as in so-called Kenotic theories. Anything so contrived or artificial would simply be inappropriate to the Christian conviction that. . .the incarnation is a positive filling, not a negative emptying: and, as such, it should, strictly speaking, constitute nothing for surprise, as though it were something incongruous with God's majesty, however much it may be a theme for adoring wonder as congruous with God's eternal, generous self-giving.[22]

Another way of expressing what is, I think, *partially* the same view is to think with Frank Weston (subsequently Bishop of Zanzibar) of the two 'states' of the Logos/Son in terms of 'sums of relationships'. Surely, he argues, 'the word state in this connection means nothing more than the sum of relationships of the Logos. On the one hand He lives in universal creative relationships with the whole of His creation, such relations being based upon His own eternal relation to the Father. On the other hand He lives on earth in special, redemptive relationships. . .based upon a new, limited, human relation to His Father. But He himself is one and the same person.'[23] So 'the Person who became incarnate is purely divine. In His eternal essence He is of one substance with the Father, God of God; possessed of all divine powers, prerogatives, and attributes. His incarnation in no way interfered with His true life in the eternal

---

[22] 'The Manhood of Jesus in the New Testament' in *Christ, Faith and History,* pp. 97ff.
[23] *The One Christ,* (Longmans, Green & Co., London, 1907), p. 147.

Godhead, or hindered Him from His divine activities in the universe. He remained true Word of God, upholding all things by the word of His power.'[24]

But, except in his sinlessness, the manhood he assumed was 'like ours, having the same natural weaknesses and limitations that hinder us', for 'he was content to accept the limitations that are proper to and normal in man. . . .'[25]

> He has *as Incarnate* no existence and no activity outside the conditions that manhood imposes upon Him. . . Hence it seems to follow of necessity that as Incarnate the Son has no communion with His Father except through the same medium of manhood. He holds communion with His Father through His human soul. For He is one person; and His manhood is, in the fullest sense, His own nature, although it is assumed. He took it to Himself not as an external organ. . .but as the very true and real nature through and in which He might mediate between God and men. It is not enough that the mediator be in contact with our nature; He must make it really and entirely His own.'[26]

Weston insists, moreover, that the sphere in which the eternal Son 'restrains himself' is that of his 'universal activities', while in the sphere of the incarnation 'the self-limited Logos can at every moment exercise only such powers as manhood may mediate'. And he adds:

> I do not mean for a moment that the two spheres can be figured as concentric circles: for that would be to lend to the Incarnate the aid of deity apart from the limitations of humanity. But I do mean that the two spheres touch, meeting in the person of the eternal Son. . .[27]

[24] *Op. cit.*, pp. 135f.
[25] *Op. cit.*, p. 138.
[26] *Op. cit.*, pp. 140f. My italics.
[27] *Op. cit.*, pp. 145-147.

As incarnate, 'the Son necessarily has a knowledge of Himself, in His relations Godward and manward, that does not belong to His universal life as Logos. The Incarnate is the Son of God existing only under conditions of manhood.' So he 'did not know Himself as God the Son possessed of and exercising unlimited power.' Again, he did not know himself 'as merely a man'; for that he was not. Nor did he know himself 'as divine-human in composite consciousness'. Instead, 'He was conscious of Himself as God-in-manhood' and knew himself 'only so far as His human soul could mediate that knowledge. But all the while in His universal state He was, nay is, the unlimited Logos who wills to be. . .in such special relations of love to the redeemed that, in the sphere in which He meets with them, He is prepared to accept this limited content of self-consciousness.'[28] So Weston concludes that 'so long as the external limits of the sphere of the Incarnation are as real as those of our manhood, so long will the person who lives within them be as really subject to manhood as we are' – sharing our human experience and human temptations, and providing us with a human example.[29] All this was written in 1907; but it is significant that seventy years later much of it is echoed in Professor E. L. Mascall's latest book, where he insists that 'the whole of the incarnate life is the life of God-made-man, and Christ's acts are the acts of God-in-manhood. Some of them may show more clearly than others that the personal subject of these acts is not a man but God; none of them, however, are acts of the divine nature acting independently of the human, for any such acts would, like the act by which the divine Word sustains the universe, fall outside the sphere of the incarnate life altogether.'[30]

Weston concludes this part of his book by emphasising that 'the manhood of Christ is His proper, assumed nature to all eternity. The state of the Incarnation is permanent. "Jesus Christ the same yesterday, today and for ever." . . .

---

[28] *Op. cit.*, p. 152f.
[29] *Op. cit.*, pp. 168-173.
[30] *Theology and the Gospel of Christ*, pp. 180f.

Thus to all eternity the Incarnate lives in and under the conditions of a glorified humanity, unburdened it is true by the earthly limitations of humanity, yet still in some sense limited. . .' For there 'remained after the ascension just those limitations that are the measure of the ultimate difference between Godhead and manhood: limitations which we lose sight of perhaps as our eyes are dazzled by the divine glory, but which none the less are real and permanent. . .' This is one of the many reasons why the extreme Kenotic position is untenable.[31]

5.   It seems to me, moreover, that we can easily exaggerate the gulf – vast though it certainly is – between God and man. Man, the Bible repeatedly affirms, was made 'in the image and likeness of God'; and that image has never been wholly defaced, in spite of the Fall. The insistence of many theologians today 'that humanity and deity are not only diverse in their metaphysical basis but are also radically incompatible' is, as Mascall remarks, wide open to challenge from the angle both of man and God. When Knox declares that is 'impossible, by definition, that God should become man', he is guilty, Mascall insists, of pushing logical deduction too far; for if there is adequate reason to believe that God did in fact become man in Jesus, then it follows that 'man is what the eternal God could become', and that 'God, the Creator, *can,* without losing his own identity, become a being of an order radically different from his own. A donkey cannot become man, nor can an angel; but God can'.[32] It is, no doubt, peculiarly appropriate to the Son to become incarnate; and human nature is the 'peculiarly appropriate', or even 'uniquely possible', nature for him to become incarnate in.[33] This seems to be implicit, at least, in Hebrews 2; and Mascall remarks that, 'so far from human nature having an inbuilt metaphysical repugnance to its assumption by God, it is precisely in such assumption that it receives

---

[31] *Op. cit.,* pp. 174-177.
[32] *Theology and the Gospel of Christ,* pp. 130f.
[33] *Op. cit.,* p. 149.

its highest self-expression and fulfilment.'[34] He insists, moreover, that 'the total dependence of created human beings on the uncreated self-existent deity makes the incarnation of God the Son in human nature not impossible or unfitting, but wholly right and proper. It is indeed supremely wonderful and unpredictable, but that is ˙another matter.'[35]

6.   Now there can be little or no doubt that the noblest quality in human nature is man's ability to love; and the New Testament unequivocally affirms that 'God is love'. But love always involves the risk – indeed, in a fallen world, almost the certainty – of suffering. So this inevitably raises the question of the alleged 'impassibility' of God. It is manifestly inadequate to suggest that it was only the human nature of Jesus which suffered in the garden, on the cross, and when he wept over Jerusalem, for it was the whole person who underwent these experiences. Nor can we confine the concept of divine suffering to the human life of the incarnate Lord who 'learnt obedience in the school of suffering'; for the yearning love of God for his wayward people is clearly revealed in the book of Hosea and in many other parts of the Old Testament, and found its fullest expression when he 'did not spare his own Son but gave him up for us all' (Rom. 8:32) and sent him 'to be the propitiation for our sins' (1 John 4:10).

But the term passibility, Professor Oliver Quick insisted, can be used in three different senses. *External* passibility refers to the relations of one being towards another, or the capacity to be acted on from outside oneself. *Internal* passibility, on the other hand, refers to those fluctuating emotions and moods which a man experiences within himself. And *sensational* passibility denotes the capacity to experience pleasure and pain, joy and sorrow.[36] In the

---

[34] *Op. cit.,* p. 167.
[35] *Op. cit.,* p. 181.
[36] I have taken these references from some as yet unpublished lectures given in Oxford, for the loan of which I am indebted to Professor Donald MacKinnon.

second or 'internal' sense, passibility cannot be postulated of God, who, as the Thirty-Nine Articles of the Church of England put it, is 'without body, parts, or *passions*'; but it was integral to the experience of the incarnate Lord, who had a human soul as well as a human body. In the 'external' and 'sensational' senses, moreover, it is no doubt true that God is impassible in the sense of not being subject to external constraint; but Mascall points out that Galot makes a distinction between 'the necessary order of God's being and the free order of his will', and suggests that 'immutability and impassibility belong to the former, but creation and redemption to the latter, in which love and suffering are really and not just verbally implicated. "In God suffering belongs not to the order of necessity and of essence, but to that of free initiative". This involves no imperfection in God; just the opposite. "He is sovereign, and sovereignty consists in acting in the freest manner, and in *not* being imprisoned in an inaccessible attitude".'[37] Of course God, as God, cannot suffer physically or die; and this was one reason why he had to become incarnate. But God himself suffers when we sin, and he suffered more than we can begin to understand when, in Christ, he 'reconciled the world to himself'. To take any other view would be to substitute the God of Islam for the God and Father of our Lord Jesus Christ, for Muslims depict Allāh as so utterly transcendent and self-sufficient that he cannot be made sad by man's rebellion, selfishness and sin or glad by his repentance and faith. In Christian or Jewish terms, however, a God who is incapable of feeling is a philosophical abstraction, not the God of the Bible. To argue that the experience of pain or sorrow is evil in itself, Quick insists, is without foundation, for neither pain nor pleasure is good or evil *in se*. 'Everything depends upon the cause of the particular pleasure or pain'; so 'it is intrinsically good to have a due sensitiveness in regard to what is intrinsically evil and this sensitiveness directly involves pain'. But the fact remains that

---

[37] Cf. Mascall, *op. cit.*, pp. 182f.

God is essentially active, not passive; so in him 'pain or sorrow is never a mere suffering, but rather a moment in the victorious activity of his love which is his joy'.[38]

7. Even in the 'Essential Trinity', moreover, we can, I think, discern a certain element of priority and what may, perhaps, be termed 'subordination'. The Bible almost always speaks in terms of a certain priority residing in, and an initiative being taken by, the Father – or, simply, by 'God'. It is God who 'so loved the world that he sent his only Son'; the Father who 'did not spare his own Son, but delivered him up for us all'; and the Son, 'who is in the bosom of the Father', who has made the Father known. The Son is in no sense a created being, for he partakes fully in the nature of the Godhead: in him, indeed, 'all the fullness of God was pleased to dwell'. But the very title Son suggests generation, derivation and a certain subordination together with identity of essence – which is, presumably, the meaning of the concept of the 'eternal generation of the Son'.[39]

Man, on the other hand, is a creature, not the Creator; and it is of the very nature of the creature to be dependent on the Creator – the God in whose hand is his 'life, and breath and all things'. So when the 'Word became flesh', and the Son became incarnate in 'the man Christ Jesus', I believe that he became what man *should* always have been – utterly dependent on his Father for everything. It is, moreover, in John's Gospel – the Gospel which testifies most explicitly to Jesus' claim to divine Sonship -- that we find this utter dependence most consistently and insistently expressed. This can be summed up in what Dodd calls 'the parable of the Apprentice', in John 5:19 f: 'A son can do nothing on his own; he does only what he sees his father doing: what father does,

---

[38] *Loc cit.*

[39] As Professor Tasker puts it, in his comment on John 14:28: 'The words "greater than I" were frequently appealed to by the Arians to support their doctrine of the creaturely subordination of the Son to the Father. They do not, however, mean that the Father is greater in power or divinity, but. . .that He that is begotten is secondary to Him who begets.' *The Gospel according to St. John* (Tyndale Press, London, 1960), p. 173.

son does; for a father loves his son and shows him all his trade.'[40] But the same refrain comes again and again: 'I cannot act by myself; I judge as I am bidden'; 'The teaching that I give is not my own; it is the teaching of him who sent me'; 'He who sent me speaks the truth, and what I have heard from him I report to the world'; 'I do nothing on my own authority, but in all that I say, I have been taught by my Father'; 'I do not speak on my own authority'; 'The word you hear is not mine: it is the word of the Father who sent me'; 'I love the Father, and do exactly as He commands.'[41] In D. M. MacKinnon's words: 'That which is represented as coming into the world in Jesus, as transcribed in the conditions of his ministry into forms of speaking his Father's words and "doing the will of Him that sent me", is what eternally he is.'[42]

8.   This is a point which Weston, I think, does not adequately emphasise; but, to me, it is *the* secret of the Incarnation: that, when God revealed himself as a man among men, the incarnate Son was utterly and completely dependent on his Father. There was nothing in this which was essentially alien to his pre-existent state, and there was nothing which was not utterly 'human', for that is how man *ought* always to have lived. Jesus could still say 'I and my Father are one' (John 10:30), but he had become man, and was living as man should have lived. He had to learn as we have to learn, for this was his Father's will; and his knowledge was limited to what he so learnt except in so far as it pleased his Father to give him some special insight or revelation – as, indeed, he does to *some* degree with others – to teach him what he would not otherwise have known. It is this which, to me, explains his ignorance about the date of the Second Advent (and, indeed, a multitude of other things, for he was a real baby, a real boy and a real

---

[40] C. H. Dodd, 'A Hidden Parable in the Fourth Gospel', in *More New Testament Studies* (Manchester University Press, 1968), pp. 30f.

[41] John 5:30; 7:16; 8:26 and 28; 10:18; 12:45 and 49f.; 14:24 and 31.

[42] D. M. MacKinnon, 'The Relation between the Doctrines of the Incarnation and the Trinity', in *Creation, Christ and Culture* (ed. R. J. McKinney, 1976), pp. 96f.

man) while yet having a unique filial consciousness, a knowledge of men, events and the future which at times went well beyond the ordinary, and the ability to speak, at his Father's prompting, words which were utterly true and authoritative, for his teaching was not his own, but his Father's. There were *many* things that his Father did not tell him, but all that he did tell him was true. This secret also explains both his authority and his vulnerability. His 'self-submission to these conditions,' as Professor MacKinnon has insisted in a broadcast talk, 'is to be seen not as an abdication of divine omnipotence but rather as its only authentic human manifestation.' While, moreover, in the 'Essential Trinity' Father and Son are not to be thought of as having distinct and individual wills, since they are one in the unity of the Godhead, the incarnate Son had a human will as well as a human body and *psyche,* and a truly human shrinking from the agony, physical and spiritual, of the cross. But his human will was wholly subject to that of his Father – at a cost we cannot begin to understand.

9. To ask whether Jesus could not sin, or rather was able not to sin, is essentially to ask the wrong question. For simply to say that he could not sin because he was God would leave us with the impression of a conscious invulnerability which would take the sting out of temptation and erect a barrier between his experience and ours; yet it is clear that if he *had* sinned he would not have been God incarnate, or even the perfect revelation of God.[43] But surely the fact is that he suffered temptation which was as real, poignant and agonising as any one has ever known, for he was allowed by his Father to drink the cup of temptation and suffering to its dregs. Only one who has been tempted in

---

[43] It is here, moreover, that we find the answer to the common question: 'Could Jesus have come down from the cross?' Like the question about whether he could sin, this is ill-conceived. Instead of the answer being either 'No, being man, he could not' *or* 'Yes, being God, he could', the answer is 'No, *being who he was,* he could not have done so, because it would have been contrary to his character, his nature, his love for mankind, and obedience to his Father's will'. It would also, of course, as Weston puts it, to have been to act outside the limitations of the humanity he had assumed.

all points as we are, and has learnt obedience in the school of
suffering, could be our example, inspiration and 'High
Priest'. But one who failed at any point, or was completely
human *'and no more'* – man, that is, not only in a positive
sharing in human genes, human *psyche,* and human experience, but in the negative sense that he was in no real
sense God – could never save us. 'A Saviour *not quite God* is
a bridge broken at the farther end,' Bishop Handley Moule
once wrote;[44] while 'a Saviour – and an Exemplar – *not
quite man* is a bridge broken at the nearer end,' as F. F.
Bruce has remarked. How Jesus could be both truly man
and truly God is the mystery of the Incarnation; but nothing,
and no one, else would suffice.

10.   It seems to me, moreover, that on this view the
exaltation presents no major problem. The Son was always,
in some sense, subordinate to the Father, although of the
very essence of the Godhead; and he was always the Word or
self-revelation of God, in nature and to men. At the Incarnation he became Jesus of Nazareth, who lived a truly human
life to make the invisible God known to men, and then died a
truly human death to reconcile us to the God who loves us so
much that he 'sent his Son to be the propitiation for our
sins'. During his earthly life he was utterly dependent on his
Father, as all men *ought* to be; and he revealed his Father to
men to the fullest extent that God can be 'manifest in the
flesh'. Then, at the exaltation, he did not cease to be
recognisably human, although no longer subject to the
limitations of terrestrial life. He is still, today, the 'friend of
sinners', our elder brother; and our great High Priest is still
'touched with the feeling of our infirmities'. It is the fact that
he is still man as well as God which makes his intercession
for us understandable and meaningful. But he is also the
Lord whom we rightly worship and may rightly address in
prayer. It is 'in the face of Jesus Christ' that we can now see
something of the *shekinah* glory, although only 'darkly, as in

---

[44]   Prefatory Note to Sir R. Anderson *The Lord from Heaven* (1910) p. vi.

a mirror'; but one day we shall 'see him as he is' and at last be 'conformed to his likeness' – and then 'God will be all in all'.

11.   Meanwhile, we confess that 'Jesus is Lord'; the 'only Absolute in the midst of a thousand relativities'; the Alpha and Omega, who is the same 'yesterday, today and for ever'. And it is not only his present exaltation, but his sufferings, which speak to our condition. As Edward Shillito wrote, after the first World War:

If we have never sought, we seek Thee now;
    Thine eyes burn through the dark, our only stars;
We must have sight of thorn-pricks on Thy brow,
    We must have Thee, O Jesus of the Scars.

The heavens frighten us; they are too calm;
    In all the universe we have no place.
Our wounds are hurting us; where is the balm?
    Lord Jesus, by Thy Scars, we claim Thy grace.

The other gods were strong; but Thou wast weak;
    They rode, but Thou didst stumble to a throne;
But to our wounds only God's wounds can speak,
    And not a god has wounds, but Thou alone.

But they must be *God's* wounds, if they are to heal – and that brings us back to the mystery of the Incarnation

Glossary

A Skeleton Glossary and Index of a few of the theological terms used in this book.

Apollinarianism. This heresy owes its name to Apollinarius of Laodicea (b. about 310 A.D.), who taught that in the incarnate Christ the place of the human mind (*nous* or *pneuma*), which is the directing principle in human life (and therefore leads men into sin), was taken by the divine Logos. So Christ was not a true man, but partook of part only of our nature. Cf. pp. 47-48, 51-54, 130.

Adoptionism. This is an umbrella term for a number of different theories according to which Jesus was a man on whom divine qualities were conferred and who was thus 'adopted' as the Divine Word and Son of God—whether at his baptism, his resurrection, or some other time. Cf. pp. 24-27, 37, 83-86, 93, 95, 103, etc.

Apologists are those who defend the faith against those who deny or pervert it. But the term is used in this book primarily for men like Justin Martyr and Athenagoras who tried, in the second and third centuries, to correct misrepresentations of the Christian faith and to explain it to their educated contemporaries in a way they would be able to understand. Cf. pp. 41-42.

Arianism was condemned as heretical at the Council of Nicaea. The views of Arius are, perhaps, explained in sufficient detail (for the purpose of this book) on pp. 30, 40, 43-45, 51-52, 130.

Avatars. A term used by Hindus for 'descents' of the gods to the earth in the form of a man or even an animal. They resemble a theophany, or an 'appearance' of God (or one of the gods) in human form, rather than a genuine incarnation. Cf. pp. 61-63, etc.

Binitarianism. A word used of tendencies to think or speak of the Godhead in two-fold rather than trinitarian terms. Sometimes it represents a relic of those early days when it was the exalted Lord Jesus who was instictively identified with God before the trinitarian doctrine had been formulated, while sometimes it is an echo of views in which the Son and the Spirit were confused or identified. Cf. pp. 37, 38, 41, etc.

Docetism represents the attitude of those who believed that Jesus Christ was not a real, historical man but only *seemed* to be. And the term 'psychological docetism' is a convenient label for those who still so emphasise his essential deity as to minimise his genuine humanity. Cf. pp. 30-31, 35-37, 45, 47-48, 51, 54, 62, 93, 98-99, 130, etc.

Eutychianism. Eutyches (circ. 378-454) was an early Monophysite (q.v.) who acknowledged 'two natures' in Christ 'before the union', but only one nature thereafter—when, in effect, the human nature was subsumed in the divine. Cf. p. 50, etc.

158

Economic trinitarianism. This is a less extreme form of Modalism (q.v.). Instead of speaking of 'modes' it describes the differentiations within the Godhead as 'economies' or 'dispensations' for the purposes of creation and redemption. Like Modalism, the major emphasis is always on the divine unity (cf. Monad, monist); but the economies were accepted as permanent from the time of their extrapolation. Cf. pp. 39-40, 142. Contrast Tritheism.

Gnosticism is an umbrella term for several systems of thought and teaching which professed to convey to men a special knowledge (*gnōsis*) of God and his ways and claimed that this esoteric knowledge was itself the essence of 'salvation'. Cf. pp. 16, 36-37, 45, 51, 130, etc.

Gnostic Docetism emphasised the immense distance between the ineffable Godhead and his human creatures, and the paramount need for some intermediary or intermediaries who are neither fully God nor simply man. On one such view 'the Ungenerated Father sent his firstborn Mind (Christ) to free those who believe in him from the power of those who made the world. He did not [himself] suffer, but Simon of Cyrene was crucified instead'. (*A Dictionary of Christian Theology*, p. 135). Cf. pp. 36-37, 45, 51, 130.

Hypostasis. This is an elusive word which can be translated in a number of different ways: e.g. 'essence', 'entity', 'subsistence', etc. When applied to the Trinity it came to be used of those personal distinctions which exist within the one substance or essence of the Godhead, while in christological debate it was primarily used in the argument that both Christ's divine and human natures must be predicated of an appropriate *hypostasis,* 'primary substance, or entity, yet there could not be two *hypostases* in one 'Person'. Hence the slogan 'no nature (*physis*) without a *hypostasis*' or 'no *physis anhypostatos*'—slogans which played their part in giving rise to the doctrine of the 'impersonal humanity' of the incarnate Lord. Leontius of Jerusalem tried to solve this problem by postulating that the human nature of Christ found its *hypostasis* in that of the Logos, so it was not *anhypostatos* but *enhypostatos*. Cf., in this context, pp. 38-39, 48-49, 51, 53-54, 91, 102, 130-131, 134,—but especially, pp. 145-146.

Impassibility. The Greeks insisted that God can neither change nor suffer. He is 'impassable'. But this *cannot* be postulated, in these unqualified terms, of the God portrayed in the Bible. Cf. pp. 44, 46, 50, 131, etc., and especially pp. 151-153, 155 and 157. In so far as the incarnate Lord is concerned, much the same principles apply to the content, and limits, of his human knowledge, and to the reality of his temptations. Cf. pp. 50, 146-149, 153-157.

Kenōsis, Kenotic Theory, etc. These are, I think, sufficiently explained (for the purpose of this book) on pp. 49, 57-59, 131-135 and 146-150.

Kerygma. This is the technical term commonly used for the Apostolic proclamation, or the substance of what they preached. Cf. pp. 15, 16, 60, 67.

Manichaean. The word derives from Manes, a Persian of the third century. His teaching was an advanced form of Persian Dualism; he regarded matter as being, *par se,* intrinsically evil; and he taught a rigid asceticism. Cf. p. 16.

Modalism. This is an extreme form of trinitarian doctrine which emphasises the divine Unity at the expense of the Divine plurality. The One God is substantial, the three differentiations adjectival. They are 'modes of manifestation' or relevation, rather than subsisting relations or centres of consciousness. A primary weakness in Modalism is that it allows no scope for any essential love *within* the triune God and thus makes him dependent on his creation in order to manifest his essential character. Cf. pp. 38-40, 142; and contrast Tritheism.

Monarchianism, in its different forms, is perhaps sufficiently explained (for the purposes of this book) on pp. 37-40 and 42.

Monism, in its extreme Hindu form, affirms that there is only one Reality, and that all else is illusion. In the history of Christian thought many of those with monist tendencies have become Unitarians. Others do not repudiate the Trinity, but put their major emphasis on the divine Unity. In Christology, again, those with monist leanings emphasise the unity of Christ's person, while so-called 'dualists' stress his 'two natures'. In its extreme form the monist emphasis has led to the Apollinarian and Eutychian heresies, and the dualist tendency to Nestorianism. Cf. pp. 38-44, 46-50, 51-52, 59.

Monophysites were those who, even after the Definition of Chalcedon, continued to regard Christ's human nature as subsumed in the divine, and called their opponents Dyophysites because of their belief in *two* natures. Similarly, the term *Monothelites* was used of those who emphasised that the incarnate Lord had only one will—and that, necessarily, divine; and they used the term *Dyothelites* of those who insisted that the man Christ Jesus *must* also have had a human will, although this was always kept subject to that of his Father. Cp. pp. 55-56, 154-155.

Nestorianism was a form of teaching attributed (perhaps mistakenly) to Nestorius, but largely derived from Theodore of Mopsuestia. It was distinctively 'dualist' in making as clear-cut a distinction as possible between the divine and human in Christ, and was condemned as heretical. Nestorius objected, in particular, to the use of the title Theotokos ('Mother of God') in relation to the Virgin Mary. So the Definition of Chalcedon explicitly states that Christ was 'begotten of the Father before the ages as to his Godhead, and in the last days, the same, for us and our salvation, of Mary the Virgin, Theotokos, as to his manhood'. Cf. pp. 48-50, 52-53, 55 and 59.

Sarx is the Greek word for 'flesh'. It is used in the New Testament in several senses, but particularly both for human nature in general ('the Word was made flesh') and also (especially by St Paul) for the sinful principle in human nature which 'strives' against the Spirit. Cf. pp. 36, 46 and 47.

Soteriology. This is the technical term for the doctrine of salvation. It covers the fall of man, the teaching about sin, God's redemptive work and its culmination in the Atonement. Cf. pp. 20, 137-139.

Index

161